LUKE

Spiritual Commentaries on the Bible

New Testament Editor

Mary Ann Getty-Sullivan

John Gillman

LUKE

Stories of Joy and Salvation

New City Press

Published in the United States by New City Press
202 Cardinal Rd., Hyde Park, NY 12538
©2002 John Gillman

Cover design by Nick Cianfarani

Library of Congress Cataloging-in-Publication Data:

Gillman, John.
    Luke : stories of joy and salvation / John Gillman.
        p. cm. -- (Spiritual commentaries on the Bible)
        1. Bible. N.T. Luke--Commentaries. I. Title II. Series.

    BS2595.53 .G55 2002
    226.4'07-dc21   2002025522

Printed in Canada

Contents

Introduction

Anyone who reads through the Gospel of Luke with an open heart to the living Jesus will not be disappointed. Through his saving actions and words, Jesus, God's beloved, serves as a faithful guide on our spiritual journey. Indeed, for the Christian Jesus is to be the very center of our quest for union with God.

Many, especially those who suffer because of their fidelity to God's prophet, will find in Luke's story of Jesus a source of comfort in the midst of daily struggles. Others, whose lives are controlled by the pursuit of personal gain, wealth, and power, may well be deeply challenged, even disturbed by listening to the Lukan Jesus. All those who are seeking spiritual joy and peace will discover, if open to the working of the Spirit, which path to take and whom to follow as they listen attentively to Luke's narrative of Jesus.

This commentary is intended to serve as a guide to the Gospel. Most gospel passages are included, each followed by reflections on the text and a brief meditation. The reader is encouraged to engage the entire Gospel, not overlooking those sections that have been left out due to space limitations. If you find the meditations to be pertinent to your current life situation, allow them to point you back to the living Word of God for further insight and transformation. Working through the Gospel of Luke as a spiritual exercise, you may want to keep a journal, noting your own thoughts, feelings and aspirations.

Background

Who wrote the Third Gospel? What place does it have in the New Testament? To begin with the second question, we note several connections between the Gospel of Luke and the Acts of the Apostles. Both are dedicated to Theophilus (Lk 1:1–4; Acts 1:1–3), are written with much the same literary style, and are composed with similar theological themes in mind, e.g., salvation history presented as a part of human history (Lk 1:5; 2:1–2; 3:1–2; Acts 4:5-6;11:28; 18:2,12). For, as Paul boldly attests to the Roman procurator Festus, "this was not done in a corner" (Acts 26:26). Luke-Acts then are to be read and understood as a single literary work written by the same author. For us this means that each of the two parts, Luke and Acts, can help us interpret the other.

Now about the author. Who is this gifted story teller and artistic theologian we encounter? Nowhere in the text is the writer identified. Placed between Mark and John in the New Testament, the Third Gospel has been known as the Gospel according to Luke since the end of the second century. Paul names one of his fellow workers "Luke" (Phlm 24; see 2 Tm 4:11) and Colossians 4:14 refers to "Luke the beloved physician." Could the composer of Luke-Acts be this Luke known to Paul? In the Acts of the Apostles there are several passages about Paul where the author begins using "we" (16:10–17; 20:5–15; 21:1–18; 27:1–28:16), suggesting that he was a companion of that Apostle to the Gentiles. Attempts to understand the "we passages" as a fictional technique are not persuasive. This evidence leads us to concur with the traditional view that the Gospel was written by Luke, a companion of Paul.

The recipients, who were primarily Greek-speaking, Gentile Christians, probably came from diverse ethnic backgrounds, religious persuasions, social status, and economic conditions. The date of composition is after the destruction of Jerusalem in 70 C.E., alluded to in the text (see Lk 13:35; 19:43–44; 21:20). Allowing time for reflection on this event, many believe that the

10

Gospel was written between 80 and 85 C.E. The place of composition remains an open question.

Themes

There are multiple themes in Luke's Gospel. It is a Gospel of promise and fulfillment, a Gospel for the Gentiles, a Gospel featuring women and the poor. This is also a Gospel of the Holy Spirit, a Gospel of forgiveness and a Gospel of peace and joy,

As a Gospel of promise and fulfillment, Luke continually shows how God's plan of salvation is fulfilled in Jesus' suffering, death and resurrection. The frequent references to the Hebrew scriptures show how God's promises in the past are accomplished in the person of Jesus. Particularly perplexing for Luke is the rejection of Jesus by some of his own people (see Lk 2:34; 4:24; 13:31–34; 19:41–48; 23:18–31). Although there are faithful and just persons in Israel (Lk 1:5–2:28), Luke writes a Gospel open to those Gentiles, such as the Samaritans and Zacchaeus, who accept Jesus (see Lk 2:32; 10:29–37; 17:12–19; 19:1–10). Salvation is universal, open to all those who welcome God's prophet.

Luke features the role of women in his story of Jesus. Elizabeth, Mary, and Anna from the Infancy Narratives are models of faith. Jesus' mother in particular stands out as the true disciple who fully embraces God's word and courageously announces great things the Mighty One has done (1:38, 46–55; see 11:27–28). When dining with a Pharisee, Jesus commends a nameless woman for her faith (7:50); when journeying through Galilee, he is accompanied by a group of women who share their resources (8:1–3); when in the home of two sisters, he receives Martha's hospitality and commends Mary for choosing the better part (10:38–42); and when observing activity in the Temple, he commends a poor widow for her generosity (21:1–4). And finally, the first apostles of the resurrection are a group of women including Mary Magdalene, Joanna, and Mary the mother of James (24:10–11; 22–25).

Luke has a special place for the poor. To them Jesus is sent to offer glad tidings (4:18), to pronounce blessing (6:20), to invite to the great feast (14:21, 23), to bring to Abraham's bosom (16:19–31), and to welcome into paradise (23:43). This does not mean that the rich are excluded or condemned. Zacchaeus is an outstanding example of a wealthy person who joyfully accepted Jesus into his heart and home (19:1–10).

The Holy Spirit plays a prominent role in Luke's Gospel. God's spirit fills John the Baptist already from the womb (1:15), brings about the conception of Jesus in Mary (1:35), fills Elizabeth and Zechariah leading them to praise (1:41, 67), and comes upon Simeon (2:25). The Holy Spirit descends upon Jesus at his baptism (3:22), leads him into the desert (4:1), and then back to Galilee where Jesus is filled with the power of the divine Spirit (4:14). Because the Spirit of the Lord is upon him, Jesus is able to proclaim his mission (4:18–19). Jesus later rejoices in the Holy Spirit, announces that the Father gives the Spirit to those who ask (11:13), and promises that the divine Spirit will teach the disciples what to say (12:12). Finally, when Jesus dies he commends his spirit into God's hands (23:46). This same Holy Spirit is promised to believers today in every circumstance offering wisdom and strength.

More than the other Gospels, Luke's champions the theme of forgiveness. Having the authority as the Son of Man to pardon sins (5:24), Jesus pardons his persecutors (23:34), calls his followers to be reconciled with fellow believers (17:3–4), and teaches them to ask the Father for mercy (11:4). At the beginning of the Gospel, Zechariah proclaims that the prophet of the Most High brings forgiveness of sins (1:77); the Gospel ends with Jesus commissioning his disciples to preach the forgiveness of sins in his name (24:47). At the heart of the Gospel Jesus defends before Pharisees and scribes his mission to tax collectors and sinners (15:1–32). Like the shepherd who goes after the lost sheep, the woman who searches for the lost coin, and the father who welcomes back his lost son, Jesus searches out those who have gone astray and rejoices when they return.

Above all, Luke's Gospel is a story of joy, peace and salvation. The story begins in unlikely circumstances with an old and barren couple promised a child and a young single woman told that she will bear a son. Through God's power the impossible happens, bringing great joy to many—women, neighbors, and shepherds—leading them to rejoice (1:14, 44, 47, 58; 2:10). As in the case of Zacchaeus, the word of God is to be received with joy (8:13; 19: 6); even those persecuted are to leap for joy (6:23). Disciples can celebrate because their names are written in heaven (10:20). Recognizing Jesus, the Emmaus companions were incredulous with joy (24:41), and after Jesus departed the disciples returned to Jerusalem with great joy (24:52). Joy emanates from a person at peace. Jesus has given us the gift of peace (24:36), guides us into its way (1:79), instructs us to be messengers of peace (10:5–6), and sends us our way as he did the woman who showed great love: "Your faith has saved you; go in peace" (7:50).

I

Stories of Joy and Salvation
(1:1–2:52)

Luke begins his story of Jesus and the church by telling his readers what he intends to do and why (1:1–4). Then he invites us to listen to the marvels God has worked in the lives of two significant couples: Zechariah and Elizabeth, who gave birth to John the Baptist, and Joseph and Mary, who gave birth to Jesus (1:5–2:52). These closely related infancy narratives present John the Baptist as the forerunner and Jesus as the Davidic Messiah and the unique Son of God. They also introduce the major themes that Luke unfolds in the rest of the Gospel: salvation is for all peoples; peace and joy are its hallmarks; the lowly are held in special regard; women of faith play a central role in God's plan; and the Spirit of God works powerfully, often in unexpected ways.

Written for the Friend of God (1:1–4)

[1] Many have undertaken to compile a narrative of the events that have been fulfilled among us, [2] just as those who were eyewitnesses from the beginning and ministers of the word have handed them down to us. [3] I too have decided, after investigating everything accurately anew, to write it down in an orderly sequence for you, most excellent Theophilus, [4] so that you may realize the certainty of the teachings you have received.

In one long artfully crafted sentence, Luke situates himself among other ministers of the word and explains his plan. As a second or third generation believer—not an eyewitness himself—Luke draws upon the testimony of others who have handed down to him a "narrative of the events that have been fulfilled." These events are stories about Jesus by those who believed in him. The accomplished fulfillment may well be understood in a double sense. On one level, the events narrated in the Gospel fulfill previous prophecy; on another level, the events are continually being fulfilled in an ongoing way by the faith response they elicit. Luke builds upon the work of others, including the Gospel of Mark, a collection of sayings scholars commonly refer to as the Q source, and other special material, found only in this Gospel. "After investigating everything accurately anew," Luke writes his own "orderly sequence."

The person for whom Luke writes is Theophilus, a name that means "friend of God" or "lover of God." Although it is not certain, Theophilus may have been an influential person of high social standing ("most excellent") who was attracted to Jesus. Some suggest that he was Luke's patron. Theophilus may also symbolically represent any person who believes in Jesus and wants to grow in the faith. Luke's community of believers, regardless of differences in social status, are the friends of God.

Luke writes so that Theophilus might "realize the certainty of the teachings" he had received. Like readers of the Gospel through the ages, Theophilus is not hearing about Jesus for the first time. He is being supported, bolstered in his faith. Luke writes to bring Theophilus and others like him to full conviction that the Jesus story is indeed a reliable basis for life decisions. What Luke proclaims is true, it definitely is God's plan of salvation (see Acts 2:36).

For reflection: The beginning of Luke's Gospel reminds us that all who believe, or who yearn to grow in their faith, are friends of God. The spiritual life is above all else about fostering this kind of intimate relationship with the Holy One. And like Luke, Christians today believe because their faith has been handed on to them by others who stand in a long line of witnesses to the living God. From whom have you received your faith: parents, grandparents, religious leaders? How have they shared their faith with you? What stories of faith have you been told? Can you recapture the first awakening of your faith? What was that like? Looking at this from another vantage point, how have you handed on your belief to others: your children, your circle of friends, and your acquaintances?

Announcement of the Birth of Jesus (1:26–38)

[26] In the sixth month, the angel Gabriel was sent from God to a town of Galilee called Nazareth, [27] to a virgin betrothed to a man named Joseph, of the house of David, and the virgin's name was Mary. [28] And coming to her, he said, "Hail, favored one! The Lord is with you." [29] But she was greatly troubled at what was said and pondered what sort of greeting this might be. [30] Then the angel said to her, "Do not be afraid, Mary, for you have found favor with God. [31] Behold, you will conceive in your womb and bear a son, and you shall name him Jesus. [32] He will be great and will be called Son of the Most High, and the Lord God will give him the throne of David his father [33] and he will rule over the house of Jacob forever, and of his kingdom there will be no end." [34] But Mary said to the angel, "How can this be, since I have no relations with a man?" [35] And the angel said to her in reply, "The Holy Spirit will come upon you, and the power of the Most High will overshadow you. Therefore the child to be born will be called holy, the Son of God. [36] And behold, Elizabeth, your relative, has also conceived a son in her old age, and this is the sixth month for her who was called barren; [37] for nothing will be impossible for God." [38] Mary said, "Behold, I am the handmaid of the Lord. May it be done to me according to your word." Then the angel departed from her.

Luke first announces the birth of John (1:5–25), then the birth of Jesus (1:26–38). In each case the conditions for the possibility of pregnancy seem to be unlikely: Both Zechariah and Elizabeth were "advanced in years" (1:7), and Mary was a "virgin" who had "no relations with a man" (1:34). Thus, it is understandable that the initial response was one of disbelief on the part of Zechariah, John's father (1:20). Because Zechariah did not believe, he was rendered speechless until the naming of his son. Mary, Jesus' mother, was "greatly troubled" (1:29) and perplexed (1:34), though later she is praised by Elizabeth for believing what was spoken to her (1:45).

Those in Luke's community familiar with the Jewish scriptures would readily recall that in the past God brought forth a son to aged childless parents, such as Isaac to Abraham and Sarah (Gn 18:9-15; 21:1-8) and Samuel to Elkanah and Hannah (1 Sm 1-2). Hence, it is not completely unexpected that God fulfills the promise to Zechariah by bringing forth a son who would bring "joy and gladness" not only to this barren couple but to many others as well (1:14). For God is indeed a faithful God who visits his people as Zechariah later proclaims. Promises made by God become promises fulfilled, even when one's circumstances would seem to indicate otherwise.

Contrary to custom an angelic messenger, Gabriel (see Dn 8:16-26; 9:21-27), tells Zechariah and Mary what to name their sons. The meaning of these names reveals the respective roles that John and Jesus play in the drama of salvation. John, meaning "God has shown favor," is the one who "will go before the Lord to prepare his ways" (1:76). He will be "a voice of one crying out in the desert" (3:4), calling the crowds to conversion in preparation for the coming of God's beloved son (3:22). Later in the Gospel, Jesus praises John publicly and lavishly, saying: "among those born of women, no one is greater than John" (7:28). Jesus, whose name means "God saves," is the one through whom God brings healing and wholeness in the most profound sense.

The announcement of Jesus' birth follows a pattern of a divine call or a commissioning often found in biblical stories. This pattern is indicated in the following analysis by the italicized words. In the *introduction* to the scene the sending of the angel Gabriel by God to Mary is announced (1:26-27). The

17

messenger's *greeting* discloses Mary's special status: "Hail (also translated 'rejoice'), favored one! The Lord is with you" (1:28). Unexpectedly, God bestows favor on a person who is young and female—in a society that traditionally honors those who are elderly and male. One would rather expect such an honor to be given to the priest Zechariah, whose religious status affords him the privilege of entering the sanctuary of the Lord to offer incense while the people prayed outside (1:9). Yet Mary's favor is not a private matter for her alone but a great benefit to all who come to believe in her son. Unlike Elizabeth who is introduced with elevated status as coming from the priestly family of Aaron (1:5), Mary is presented without distinction or family ties, almost as an orphan.

In *reaction* to the greeting, Mary ponders its meaning and becomes "greatly troubled" (1:29). Why would such an insignificant person be singled out for God's favor? In *response*, the angel offers *reassurance*: "Do not be afraid" (1:30). Then comes the *commission* in the form of a future promise: Mary will bear a son (1:31–33). He will be called Jesus and will rule over Israel forever. Echoing the prophet Daniel, the angel proclaims that this child will be called "Son of the Most High." To this Mary offers a mild *protest*. Though betrothed, she wonders how this can be since she has had "no relations with a man" (1:34). To the reader, this would not seem to be an insurmountable obstacle, since it is possible for Mary to have relations and to conceive a child. However, this is not part of the divine plan, for the angel, again offering *reassurance*, relates that the Holy Spirit "will overshadow" her, thus conceiving a son (1:35–37). Mary's response is one of *acceptance*: "May it be done to me according to your word" (1:38). By her *fiat*, her yes, Mary becomes the model believer, and in an anticipatory way the first disciple, belonging to the family of disciples, for she hears "the word of God and acts on it" (8:21).

For reflection: God is at work bringing about something new and unexpected. Gabriel is sent, not to aged parents longing for a child, but to a young virgin who is completely surprised that she is being singled out to be the mother of Jesus, the son of God. In this call story the invitation is given, a doubt is raised, reassurance offered, followed by a response in faith. This pattern is found in the lives of many people in the Bible, such as Abraham and Sarah, Moses and Jeremiah, Deborah and Gideon. Throughout the centuries those invited to be disciples have wrestled with their vocation, doubted their worthiness and offered objections. Yet the Holy One persists in the vocation, and gives us the grace to work through our hesitations. This is a great comfort to Christians today who encounter uncertainties as they grapple with the vocation to service. Mary's response to the living God becomes a model for us all: "Be it done to me according to your word."

The Canticle of Mary (1:46–55)

46 And Mary said:
"My soul proclaims the greatness of the Lord;
47 my spirit rejoices in God my savior.
48 For he has looked upon his handmaid's lowliness;
behold, from now on will all ages call me blessed.
49 The Mighty One has done great things for me,
and holy is his name.
50 His mercy is from age to age
to those who fear him.
51 He has shown might with his arm,
dispersed the arrogant of mind and heart.
52 He has thrown down the rulers from their thrones
but lifted up the lowly.
53 The hungry he has filled with good things;
the rich he has sent away empty.
54 He has helped Israel his servant,
remembering his mercy,
55 according to his promise to our fathers,
to Abraham and to his descendants forever."

As a model believer Mary does not stay at home dwelling on her recently acclaimed favored status, but sets out on a journey to the house of Elizabeth. Through the angel Gabriel's message (1:36) Mary became aware of Elizabeth's pregnancy, with whom she then stays for three months. The two mothers meet and share their stories. Filled with the Holy Spirit, Elizabeth proclaims a threefold blessing: first Mary is called blessed among women (1:42a; see Jdt 13:18), then the fruit of her womb is declared blessed (1:42b), and finally, Mary is once again announced as blessed, this time because she believed that what was spoken to her would be fulfilled (1:45). In contrast to the disbelief of Zechariah, Mary is acclaimed as the faithful one.

Mary responds to Elizabeth's greeting in a hymn of praise that has been part of the Church's evening prayer for many centuries. The Canticle of Mary, traditionally called the Magnificat, unfolds in two parts: the first announces what God has done for Mary (1:46–50), and the second proclaims God's action in society at large (1:51–55). What God has brought about in the life of one lowly woman becomes a powerful sign of what God has done and will accomplish for the community of the lowly. Mary stands in solidarity with those who are economically, socially and politically poor.

Every verse in this hymn recalls Old Testament motifs (see especially 1 Sm 2:1–10). The Magnificat is like a carefully crafted tapestry of interwoven motifs from Israel's tradition. Acclamations of praise, acts of divine liberation, and allusions to other great women and men of faith are artfully threaded together to give a striking picture of God's gracious intervention on behalf of the oppressed in Israel.

In response to being declared blessed by Elizabeth, Mary proclaims "the greatness of the Lord" (1:46). Having herself experienced "the power of the Most High" overshadow her (1:35), Mary praises God, the primary agent of the song. The terms "my soul" and "my spirit" refer to Mary as a whole person: she "proclaims" and "rejoices." This recalls Habakkuk 3:18: "Yet will I rejoice in the Lord and exult in my saving God" (see also Ps 19:5, LXX; 40:17; and 70:5). "God my Savior" (1:47), identified as "The Mighty One" (1:49), is the divine warrior who champions the cause of the people Israel.

Echoing her previous reply to Gabriel (1:38), Mary calls herself *doulē*, a Greek term translated by the New American Bible (NAB) as "handmaid" (1:48) though it literally means "servant" or "slave." In this way Mary places herself in the household of God, under whose authority she stands. Previously called blessed by Elizabeth, this servant of God is the one who will be called blessed by all future generations in the new era of salvation inaugurated by God through her son. The "lowliness" of Mary (1:48, see Jdt 16:11) stands in contrast to the deeds of the "Mighty One." The lowliness of Mary recalls the *Anawim*, the "poor ones" of Israel. These are the ones who suffer persecution and oppression; they are God's elect and favored ones. By placing this hymn on Mary's lips, Luke makes her a spokesperson for the *Anawim*.

In the second part of the hymn the focus changes from Mary to Israel as a whole. In a series of action verbs, "show might," "dispersed," "thrown down," "filled," "sent away," and "helped," the powerful action of God is acclaimed. Showing might with "his arm" recalls God's role of deliverance in the Exodus event. The arm of God symbolizes God's power. The "arrogant" are the proud, sufficient unto themselves. "Rulers" denotes those Romans and client kings in the Gospel who wield power over the people. They will be thrown down from their thrones. These are prophetic words that promise social and political liberation for an oppressed people.

Mary portrays God as one whose mighty acts of salvation bring about a socio-political reversal. Both oppressors and oppressed have their fortunes dramatically overturned. The lowly and hungry are "lifted up" and "filled with good things." Who are the lowly and the hungry? They are those who, living in circumstances of real affliction and economic deprivation, utterly depend on God. The new eschatological order breaks in and transforms the social condition of those suffering in the present. God sees their plight and delivers them!

For reflection: Mary, far from being a meek, passive and docile handmaiden—as she is sometimes characterized in Christian tradition—is portrayed by Luke as a person who speaks with the authority of a prophet, challenging the existing social order. The "great things" God has done in the life of this young woman point to the liberating intervention of God in the lives of others. This passage reminds us not only to look for but also to listen to the prophetic voices that come from unexpected sources. This means that the prophets among us today may well include those without power, lofty titles, social standing or official religious function. The single Guatemalan mother with hungry children to feed, the committed lay minister in the parish serving faithfully in the years, and all those who identify with the "handmaid's lowliness" in their life circumstances have their own faith experience validated by how God acts in their lives. Are there not among these people prophetic voices to be heeded? Who are those whom you consider to be God's prophets today? How might the testimony of their faithful lives call for liberation of the oppressed?

The Canticle of Zechariah (1:68–79)

[68] "Blessed be the Lord, the God of Israel,
for he has visited and brought redemption to his people.
[69] He has raised up a horn for our salvation
within the house of David his servant,
[70] even as he promised through the mouth of his holy
prophets from of old:
[71] salvation from our enemies and from the hand of all
who hate us,
[72] to show mercy to our fathers
and to be mindful of his holy covenant

⁷³ and of the oath he swore to Abraham our father,
and to grant us that, ⁷⁴ rescued from the hand of
enemies,
without fear we might worship him
⁷⁵ in holiness and righteousness
before him all our days.
⁷⁶ And you, child, will be called prophet of the Most
High,
for you will go before the Lord to prepare his ways,
⁷⁷ to give his people knowledge of salvation
through the forgiveness of their sins,
⁷⁸ because of the tender mercy of our God
by which the daybreak from on high will visit us
⁷⁹ to shine on those who sit in darkness and death's
shadow,
to guide our feet into the path of peace."

The drama of salvation unfolds according to the plan announced by the angel to Zechariah. Having been told previously that the child is to be named John (1:13) and that he would be speechless until "these things take place," Zechariah writes that this new-born child is to be called "John"—to the amazement of all (1:63). Then after this period of divinely imposed silence, Zechariah's tongue is freed, and he blesses God (1:64). When all the neighbors ask: "What, then, will this child be?" Zechariah, "filled with the Holy Spirit," replies with the well-known canticle that is recited daily as part of the morning prayer of the Church.

Similar to the Magnificat, the Benedictus (Latin word for "blessed," which begins the hymn) is composed like a biblical tapestry of Old Testament verses and themes. Originally, it may have been either a Jewish or a Jewish Christian prayer, that has been taken over by Luke to celebrate's God's faithful action in the past, leading up to the powerful way God will act in the very near future through the prophet John (1:76) and Jesus, "the daybreak from on high" (1:78).

Zechariah speaks with divine authority since he is "filled with the Holy Spirit," a characteristic also used to describe his son, John (1:15), his wife, Elizabeth (1:41), Jesus (4:1), those gathered at Pentecost (Acts 2:4), Peter (Acts 4:8), Stephen (Acts 6:5; 7:55), and Paul (Acts 9:17; 13:9). Being spirit-filled Zechariah is empowered to announce God's plan of salvation.

In its narrative context, the canticle tells the reader how Zechariah blessed God (1:64, see 1:68–75) and then responds to the question asked by the neighbors: "What, then, will this child be?" (1:66, see 1:76–79). There is a shift in addressees from the third person in part one of this canticle that praises God (1:68–75) to the second person singular in the latter part that prophetically proclaims God's future action (1:76–79). The use of the first person plural throughout refers to the neighbors and all from the hill country of Judea (1:65), to the members of Luke's community as well as to readers today: "*our* salvation" (1:69), "all who hate *us*" (1:71), "*our* fathers" (1:72), "*our* father," "grant *us*" (1:73), "*we* might worship him" (1:74), "all *our* days" (1:75), "*our* God," "visit *us*" (1:78), "*our* feet" (1:79). The same merciful God who acted in the past by bringing salvation through the holy prophets will act in the future through Jesus, the dayspring from on high, to bring light to those who sit in darkness.

Echoing a line from the psalms (Ps 41:14; 72:18; 106:48), Zechariah begins by proclaiming "blessed" the God of Israel because God "has visited" his people, bringing them redemption (1:68). Though unspecified, this past visitation may refer to God's promise of a son given to childless Abraham and Sarah (cf. "the oath" to Abraham in 1:73 where the reference is to deliverance from enemies), echoed above in the story of John's birth to Zechariah and Elizabeth.

In the second part, Zechariah addresses his words to John, calling him "prophet of the Most High" (1:76, see 7:26). He announces that his mission will be to prepare the Lord's ways by giving people "knowledge of salvation," meaning "the forgiveness of sins" (1:77). This part of the canticle foreshadows John's later proclamation of a "baptism of repentance for the forgiveness of sins" (3:3). For the first time in his Gospel, Luke refers to Jesus as Lord (1:76), who is "the daybreak from on high" (1:78). The word "daybreak" is a messianic title that is used to translate the Hebrew word for "branch," referring in the Old Testament to the heir of the throne of David (Jer 23:5; Zec 3:8; 6:12).

Developing the light imagery, Zechariah's canticle concludes with a prophetic promise: the Daybreak from on high will illuminate those who are in darkness, understood as the shadow of death—the arena of cosmic forces—and will guide us "into the path of peace" (1:79). For the first time peace is used in the Gospel of Luke, a theme that will reappear in the concluding chapter as the gift of the resurrected Jesus to the startled apostles (24:36–42).

For reflection: Zechariah's canticle is rich in themes for reflection: the important role faith plays in discerning how God has brought salvation in the past and continues to bring wholeness today; the trustworthiness of God's promises—they will be fulfilled; and the focus on Jesus who is the true light guiding us from darkness and the shadow of death to the way of peace. The last of these themes is particularly poignant for us to recall when we may feel overcome with our own darkness, whether this be doubt, despair, or depression, any one of which can cause us to lose our way on our faith journey. During these times of trial it is often helpful to look back to the scriptures at the character of God who is faithful to divine promises of deliverance from enemies, whether these be external forces opposed to the Gospel or our own internal struggles. For the same God who rescued us in times past is there for us when our present journey seems fraught with obstacles of every kind. This canticle reminds us that Jesus is the one who will bring us to the highly desired state of peace.

The Birth of Jesus (2:1–14)

2:1 In those days a decree went out from Caesar Augustus that the whole world should be enrolled. ² This was the first enrollment, when Quirinius was governor of Syria. ³ So all went to be enrolled, each to his own town. ⁴ And Joseph too went up from Galilee from the town of Nazareth to Judea, to the city of David that is called Bethlehem, because he was of the house and family of David, ⁵ to be enrolled with Mary, his betrothed, who was with child. ⁶ While they were there, the time came for her to have her child, ⁷ and she gave birth to her firstborn son. She wrapped him in swaddling clothes and laid him in a manger, because there was no room for them in the inn.

⁸ Now there were shepherds in that region living in the fields and keeping the night watch over their flock. ⁹ The angel of the Lord appeared to them and the glory of the Lord shone around them, and they were struck with great fear. ¹⁰ The angel said to them, "Do not be afraid; for behold, I proclaim to you good news of great joy that will be for all the people. ¹¹ For today in the city of David a savior has been born for you who is Messiah and Lord. ¹² And this will be a sign for you: you will find an infant wrapped in swaddling clothes and lying in a manger." ¹³ And suddenly there was a multitude of the heavenly host with the angel, praising God and saying:
>   ¹⁴ "Glory to God in the highest
>   and on earth peace to those on whom his favor rests."

Gabriel's announcement of the birth of Jesus to Mary (1:26–38), and the future role of Jesus, proclaimed in Zechariah's canticle (1:78–79), lead to the story of the birth itself. Luke tells the story against the backdrop of Roman imperial power. A census of the "whole world" (i.e., Roman Empire) is decreed by the Emperor Octavian (27 B.C.E.–14 C.E.), referred to as Caesar Augustus (2:1), a title he received from the Senate in 27 B.C.E. The introduction of the high and mighty—Quirinius, the governor of Syria is also mentioned—from the political arena serves as a historical marker for one whose birth in humble circumstances is acclaimed by a heavenly figure to be savior, Messiah, and Lord (2:11).

The birth story unfolds in three parts: 1) the setting for the birth: Caesar's plan of the census and Joseph's and Mary's response of journeying to Bethlehem (2:1–5); 2) the birth itself: God's fulfillment of the promise previously made (2:6–7); and 3) the divine visitation to the shepherds and the angelic revelation of the child's identity (2:8–14). In the birth story Luke explains the meaning of this momentous event and how humans respond to it.

While Caesar Augustus is widely recognized as the one who has brought peace to the Roman world (the *Pax Romana*), Jesus is acclaimed as the Savior, the one through whom deep and lasting peace comes to the world (2:11, 14, cf. 1:79). Peace imposed by military might brought foreign domination, religious repression, and impoverishing taxation. The peace offered by Jesus the Savior brings good will among people and well being to all. Though the historical accuracy of a worldwide census is most uncertain (2:1–4), Luke emphasizes that "the events that have been fulfilled among us" (1:1) take place on the broad stage of Roman Imperial power, and not simply under Jewish kings (see the reference to Herod in 1:5). Through his decree Augustus ironically facilitates God's plan by bringing Joseph and Mary to Bethlehem, the city of David, for the birth.

Nazareth has already been established as the place where the angel Gabriel appeared to Mary (1:26), and is named here in this passage as the town where she and Joseph were living. As one of several journeys mentioned in the Gospel, this couple sets out for Bethlehem, identified as the "city of David" for it is his birthplace and original home (1 Sm 17:12-15, 58). Joseph's line of descent from the house of David will be established by Luke when he gives the genealogy of Jesus a little later in the narrative (3:23–38, see esp. v. 31).

In a surprisingly laconic fashion the birth is narrated in one verse (2:6), followed by a single verse describing Mary's parental care of the infant (2:7). Mary gives birth, wraps him, and lays him in a manger, while Joseph fades from the scene, at least until the shepherds arrive (2:16). In calling her son the "first born" rather than "only born," Luke tells us that no child was born before Jesus, and hence that Jesus had the traditional Hebrew privileges reserved to the first born (Ex 13:2; Nm 3:12–13; 18:15–16).

In a change of scenes Luke rapidly and unexpectedly takes the readers from the intimacy of the birth to a pastoral setting of shepherds in nearby fields (2:8). The movement from Caesar Augustus, far removed from and unaware of Mary's firstborn, to the lowly inhabitants in the nearby countryside, who will receive the angelic revelation, already illustrates how God is fulfilling Mary's proclamation that the lowly will be lifted up (1:52).

When an angel of the Lord appeared to the shepherds in the fields outside Bethlehem, "the glory of the Lord" shown around them (2:9). Then in solemn proclamation the angels declare: "Glory to God in the highest" (2:14). Simeon will apply this quality of the revealed presence of God specifically to Jesus when he tells Mary and Joseph that their son will be "glory for your people Israel" (2:32). Later in the narrative Peter, John, and James witness the "glory" of the transfigured Jesus (9:32), right after Jesus had announced that the Son of Man will come "in his glory and in the glory of the Father" (9:26, see 21:27). Then in the dialogue of the Emmaus story, the risen Jesus makes explicit the association between a suffering Messiah and glory, implying that it is through his suffering, that the Messiah can "enter into his glory" (24:26). The angel tells the shepherds that a "savior" has been born, and that he is "Messiah and Lord."

In Luke miraculous events are characteristically followed by an acclamation of God's praise (see 17:15–16). The peace of which the Gospel speaks includes well being, harmony in one's relationships, and security—much more than the absence of war (7:50; 8:48; 10:5–6; 19:38, 42). Peace is the pre-eminent gift brought by the risen Jesus to the troubled apostles (24:36).

For reflection: The story of Jesus' birth is interpreted by the angels with the titles Savior, Messiah, and Lord, as well as with a proclamation of peace brought by God through Jesus. It is this later gift of peace that helps us to understand what kind of Savior, Messiah and Lord, Jesus is. Contrary to the claims of those who try to get Jesus to serve their agenda, this passage reminds us that the peace God brings through Jesus is not reserved exclusively for a select group, but that God's peace is for everyone, since all enjoy God's good favor. Using Jesus to set one group against another does not reflect the spirit of this passage. In this narrative Jesus came no less for the Caesar's of this world than for the shepherds of our time. Have we allowed ourselves to receive the peace that only God can give through Jesus? And, how do we manifest this peace to others in our relationships of daily life?

The Manifestation of Jesus to Simeon and Anna (2:25–38)

²⁵ Now there was a man in Jerusalem whose name was Simeon. This man was righteous and devout, awaiting the consolation of Israel, and the holy Spirit was upon him. ²⁶ It had been revealed to him by the holy Spirit that he should not see death before he had seen the Messiah of the Lord. ²⁷ He came in the Spirit into the temple; and when the parents brought in the child Jesus to perform the custom of the law in regard to him, ²⁸ he took him into his arms and blessed God, saying:
²⁹ "Now, Master, you may let your servant go in peace, according to your word,
³⁰ for my eyes have seen your salvation, ³¹ which you prepared in sight of all the peoples,
³² a light for revelation to the Gentiles, and glory for your people Israel."

³³ The child's father and mother were amazed at what was said about him; ³⁴ and Simeon blessed them and said to Mary his mother, "Behold, this child is destined for the fall and rise of many in Israel, and to be a sign that will be contradicted ³⁵ (and you yourself a sword will pierce) so that the thoughts of many hearts may be revealed."

³⁶ There was also a prophetess, Anna, the daughter of Phanuel, of the tribe of Asher. She was advanced in years, having lived seven years with her husband after her marriage, ³⁷ and then as a widow until she was eighty-four. She never left the temple, but worshiped night and day with fasting and prayer.

³⁸ And coming forward at that very time, she gave thanks to God and spoke about the child to all who were awaiting the redemption of Jerusalem.

After the heavenly disclosure to the shepherds, they go to Bethlehem and see the child, and then spread the word to others. Eight days after his birth the parents have their child circumcised and name him Jesus, as instructed by the angel (1:31). Mary and Joseph take Jesus to the Temple in Jerusalem, where, following the Jewish legal custom of dedicating the first-born (Ex 13:2,12), they consecrate him to the Lord (2:22-23). This action recalls that part of the Samuel story where his mother, Hannah, takes him to the Temple and gives him to the priest Eli for the Lord's service (1 Sm 1:21–28).

In the Temple Simeon and Anna, two devout people, encounter the child Jesus and offer prayers of praise and blessing. These two become the fourth male and female paired together by Luke, following upon the couples Zechariah and Elizabeth in the Temple, Mary and Joseph at the birth, and Mary and Zechariah, associated on a literary level by their parallel hymns of praise. Thus, here and in the unfolding narrative, Luke gives some prominence to the roles of women alongside that of men. The connection between Simeon and Anna lies in their role as prophet and prophetess (2:25, 36), their description as devout (2:25, 37), and their prayers of blessing and thanksgiving (2:29–32; 2:38). Further, there is a striking parallel between Simeon who was "awaiting the consolation of Israel" (2:25) and Anna who addressed those "awaiting the redemption of Jerusalem" (2:38). Among those who had been waiting for the one "to redeem Israel" are the two disciples on the road to Emmaus at the end of the Gospel (24:21). The same Greek root word for redemption (*lutrōsis*) is used in both passages (2:38; 24:21).

Simeon's prophetic role is underscored by the threefold mention of the spirit in vv. 25–27: The Spirit was upon him, gave him a revelation, and accompanied him into the Temple. Being a person of the Spirit, like so many others in Luke's Gospel, his words have revelatory importance. As a prelude to the blessings he imparts, the promise-fulfillment event is highlighted. He already learned through a revelation that he would see "the Messiah of the Lord"; now this pledge is fulfilled as he holds in his arms the child of his longing (v. 28).

In a prayer blessing God, Simeon heralds several important evangelical themes conveying hope and promise, e.g., "peace," "salvation," "sight," "light," and "glory," each of which will be developed in the unfolding narrative of Luke-Acts. Particularly prominent is the proclamation of salvation for all, embracing both Gentiles and Jews, announced here for the first time in the Gospel.

While Simeon blesses both parents, he addresses troubling words to Mary about the child's destiny and the mother's pierced soul (Greek, *psyche*). The "fall and rise of many" may refer to two different groups (e.g., the "rulers" and the "lowly" mentioned in the Magnificat, 1:51), or to the same group or individual (e.g., the disciples, 24:11, 36–48; or Peter, 22:31–34; 24:12). Although unexplained in this passage, the sword that pierces Mary's inner being may be the realization that God's claim on his son will take precedence over maternal attachment (see 2:41–52; 8:19–21; 11:27–28; 23:49).

In contrast to Simeon, Anna's father and ancestral tribe are named—though not her deceased husband—thereby connecting her to her people. Her piety is portrayed as one of "fasting and prayer," a typical Lukan expression for devotion (Acts 13:3; 14:23). While Luke does not cite her words, he does say that Anna spoke "to all who were awaiting the redemption of Jerusalem." Thus, she witnesses to a broader audience about who Jesus is, in contrast to Simeon, whose words are seemingly only heard by Jesus' parents.

For reflection: Following the long tradition of the church that has included Simeon's song of praise, called the "Nunc Dimittis" (meaning "Now you can dismiss [us]") in its evening prayer, this blessing remains a rich prayer to say as each day draws to a close. Looking back over the day's events, what signs of God's saving presence have you noticed? Events that are otherwise simply regarded as rather routine, may through the eyes of faith be seen in a wholly new light. What words, perhaps a friend's expression of support during a difficult trial, or gestures, such as a caring embrace, have been signs to you of God's gracious spirit? Also, when the course of our years draws to a close, as they had for Simeon and Anna, it is helpful to look back over our life journey and to reverence those moments when God's saving hand has been there to bear us up. We may also recall those times when Simeon's words, "pierced by a sword," will have had their special relevance, times when we felt that our faith was tried and shaken. As believers we can expect, as consolation at the eventide of life, the fullness of God's light and glory to dawn upon us.

For the younger generation, the prominent role of the aged, such as Zechariah, Elizabeth, Anna, and Simeon are reminders that they often embody much spiritual wisdom. Who in your family and among your circle of acquaintances have passed on to you, often by life stories, vibrant images of faith and the shared wisdom of the believing community?

II

The Mission of John, Jesus and the Disciples
(3:1–6:11)

The drama of salvation moves rapidly from the experience of the twelve-year-old child Jesus in the Temple to his mission as an adult. But first John appears on the scene proclaiming a "baptism of repentance" (3:3) to those expecting the Messiah (3:15). During the prayer after his baptism Jesus' identity as God's "beloved son" is affirmed by the Spirit (3:22). His ancestry going back to Adam and beyond that to God, further highlights his divine sonship (3:38). The same Spirit present at Jesus' baptism leads him into the desert where he resists the threefold temptation of the devil (4:1–13), thus preparing him to proclaim the mission of healing and liberation at the synagogue in Nazareth (4:16–19). This prophetic proclamation also leads to an angry response by his own townspeople intent on hurling Jesus headlong over the brow of a hill (4:29). It now becomes painfully apparent to us that the fate of Jesus is like that of their own prophets: to be rejected by the people.

Undeterred by the plan to destroy him, Jesus astonishes the Galileans with his teaching and brings healing to a man with an unclean spirit (4:31–37), to Simon's mother-in-law (4:38–39), and to many others (4:40–41). As he travels Jesus continually proclaims the good news of the kingdom of God, for this is indeed his divine purpose (4:43). Then Jesus calls three fisherman, Simon, James, and John, to join in his mission (5:1–11). After two further healings, that of a leper (5:12–16) and a paralytic (5:17–26), Jesus calls the tax collector Levi to follow him.

Then Jesus joins him at a banquet for other tax collectors, much to the consternation of the Pharisees (5:27–32).

Concluding this section are three controversies with the Pharisees. The first dispute arises because Jesus' disciples dare to celebrate by eating and drinking instead of fasting like John's followers (5:33–39), the second because Jesus' disciples appear to break the sabbath by picking some grain on that sacred day (6:1–5), and finally because he cured a man with a withered hand on the sabbath (6:6–11). All this helps to galvanize the opposition of the religious leaders into a rage driving them to plot together "what they might do to Jesus" (6:11). Two themes emerge: Jesus' resolute faithfulness to his own mission and the hardening opposition to the very heart of this mission. By his words and actions Jesus provokes the religious establishment. His very way of being challenges their authority among the people, and thus their legitimacy.

The Preaching of John (3:1–14)

3:1 In the fifteenth year of the reign of Tiberius Caesar, when Pontius Pilate was governor of Judea, and Herod was tetrarch of Galilee, and his brother Philip tetrarch of the region of Ituraea and Trachonitis, and Lysanias was tetrarch of Abilene, 2 during the high priesthood of Annas and Caiaphas, the word of God came to John the son of Zechariah in the desert. 3 He went throughout [the] whole region of the Jordan, proclaiming a baptism of repentance for the forgiveness of sins, 4 as it is written in the book of the words of the prophet Isaiah:
"A voice of one crying out in the desert:
'Prepare the way of the Lord, make straight his paths.
5 Every valley shall be filled
and every mountain and hill shall be made low.
The winding roads shall be made straight, and the rough
ways made smooth,
6 and all flesh shall see the salvation of God.' "

⁷ He said to the crowds who came out to be baptized by him, "You brood of vipers! Who warned you to flee from the coming wrath? ⁸ Produce good fruits as evidence of your repentance; and do not begin to say to yourselves, 'We have Abraham as our father,' for I tell you, God can raise up children to Abraham from these stones. ⁹ Even now the ax lies at the root of the trees. Therefore every tree that does not produce good fruit will be cut down and thrown into the fire." ¹⁰ And the crowds asked him, "What then should we do?" ¹¹ He said to them in reply, "Whoever has two cloaks should share with the person who has none. And whoever has food should do likewise." ¹² Even tax collectors came to be baptized and they said to him, "Teacher, what should we do?" ¹³ He answered them, "Stop collecting more than what is prescribed." ¹⁴ Soldiers also asked him, "And what is it that we should do?" He told them, "Do not practice extortion, do not falsely accuse anyone, and be satisfied with your wages."

In the third and most extensive manner in three chapters, Luke relates the drama of salvation to the larger realm of worldly rulers: Zechariah's ministry occurs during the time of Herod, King of Judea (1:5); Jesus' birth takes place during the reign of Caesar Augustus (2:1), and John's preaching is dated during the imperial rule of Tiberius Caesar, various civil subordinates, and religious functionaries (3:1–2). It is unusual that both Annas and Caiphas, Annas' son-in-law, are named as high priests since normally there would be only one high priest in power at a time. It is particularly fitting that Pilate be named since he figures prominently later in the narrative (13:1; 23:1–6, 13–52; Acts 3:13; 4:27; 13:28). The repeated synchronism in Luke's opening chapters impresses upon us that what happened in a seemingly obscure corner of the Roman Empire has universal implications not to be missed.

The "word of God" comes to John (3:2), and this establishes him as a prophet. In his prophetic role John is one who proclaims a baptism of repentance (3:3) and who preaches "good news to the people" (3:18) preparing them for the prophetic Messiah who is to come after him. Later Jesus will use the image of the seed to illustrate the importance of hearing the word of God and embracing it "with a generous and good heart" (8:11,15).

Fulfilling the role that his father Zechariah previously announced for him (1:77), John proclaims "a baptism of repentance for the forgiveness of sins" (3:3). He calls for a specific ritual action of washing that symbolizes a change in behavior. The term *metanoia*, translated as repentance, literally means a change of mind or outlook. A change in thinking is necessary to bring about the kind of modifications in behavior that John will require of the crowds, the tax collectors and the soldiers a few verses later. A first step in *metanoia* is to admit one's moral failings and to seek forgiveness (*aphesis*, more broadly meaning "release" or "liberty," see 4:18). John's proclamation of the need for conversion and forgiveness of sins is reiterated at the end of the Gospel by the Risen Lord as the essential message to be carried forth by his witnesses (24:47; see Acts 2:38; 5:31).

Citing Isaiah 40:3–5, John calls for a transformation of the landscape so that a straight royal road can be prepared for when the ruler enters into the city: "Prepare the way of the Lord, make straight his paths" (3:4). The salvation of God is for "all flesh" (3:6), embracing Gentiles, tax collectors and sinners, echoing the universal theme sounded previously by Simeon (2:30–32). The optimism John communicates here does not make him a tepid preacher, for he goes on to upbraid the crowds with the invective "You brood of vipers!" (3:7). It is a wonder that they do not go for his throat then, as the furious townspeople later go after Jesus (4:28). John is not so lucky, however, when he later charges Herod Antipas for "all the evil deeds" he committed. For Herod summarily puts him in prison (3:19-20). But before that happens John charges the crowds to produce good fruit, an image for praiseworthy human behavior (3:8; see 6:43; 8:8; 13:6–9; see 20:9–16). Failure to respond brings evil consequences in the present for "even now the ax lies at the root of the trees" (3:9).

As John captures his hearers' attention, the crowds, tax collectors, and soldiers inquire: "What then should we do?" (3:10,12,14). This a question about salvation, bringing either life or death, a question raised later by the rich man (18:18), and then by the Pentecost crowd in Jerusalem listening to Peter (Acts 2:37). Peter replies to them as the Baptist would: "Repent and be baptized . . . for the forgiveness of your sins" and specifically requires that this is to be done "in the name of Jesus Christ" (Acts 2:38).

To the crowd's query, John commands: "Whoever has two cloaks should share with the person who has none. And whoever has food should do likewise" (3:11). The term *chitōn*, translated by the NAB as "cloak" more properly means undergarment. Normally a peasant would have two such tunics, one for the sabbath and one for daily use. Yet even the person with so little is required to share. Because of their own experience of want, the poor sharing with the poor creates a special kind of solidarity. If even the destitute are called to share with others, how much more so are the wealthy, like the rich man (16:19–31) and Zacchaeus (19:2) mentioned later. While the former refuses to share with poor Lazarus, the latter responds generously.

The tax collectors are not told to abandon their profession but are commanded not to collect more than the legal tolls and custom duties. The system was that the right to collect taxes was auctioned off to the highest bidder, who in turn would be driven to extort as much as possible from the populace to clear a large profit. John implies that dishonesty is common among tax collectors and that this has to cease. He does not call for upturning the social order but for bringing moral responsibility to existing professions.

Then come the soldiers. During the Baptist's generation these would be Jewish men enlisted in the service of Herod

Antipas, one of the sons of Herod the Great. John gives them a threefold instruction: Do not extort, do not accuse falsely for gain, and be satisfied with your pay. He warns them against economic exploitation of others and discontent regarding their wages. With possibly one exception, in the rest of his narrative Luke refers to Roman centurions and soldiers positively as open to Jesus and the Gospel. The centurion who comes to Jesus is commended for his faith (7:1–10), the centurion at the cross proclaims Jesus' innocence (23:47), and the centurion Cornelius believes and is baptized (Acts 10:1–49). One of Cornelius' soldiers is called "devout" (Acts 10:7), and nothing further is said about the soldier who guarded Paul under house arrest (Acts 28:16), but one can imagine that Paul spoke to him about the Gospel.

For reflection: John is a bearer of good news to the people (3:18), and his good news is about the one mightier than he who is to come. On their own spiritual journey Christians today can often identity a spiritual mentor or guide who has had a significant influence in planting the seeds of faith and offering wise counsel along the way. Maybe this is one's parents, a grandparent, a godparent, a pastor, a teacher, or a friend. That person who taught us how to pray, that person who shared spiritual wisdom that we regularly remember during times of crisis would be the John the Baptist in our life. If you like to use a journal as a part of your prayer it would be a good practice to name the spiritual guides in your life and to recall how each has influenced you through word and deed. What have they said that you remember? What good fruit from their life gives you courage to bear good fruit in yours? Also developing a spirit of gratitude for these mentors is important. Albert Schweitzer, the gifted musician, theologian, and philosopher, who became a physician to so many at Lambaréné in Gabon, Africa, often said that he wished he had taken the opportunity to express his thanks to the many who guided him in his younger years.

Divine Affirmation of Jesus after his Baptism (3:21–22)

It is only after John is imprisoned and thus taken off the narrative stage, at least for a time, that the adult Jesus emerges. Nothing is said about an encounter between Jesus and John nor any dialogue between them. In a short passage of two verses, Luke, following Mark, narrates not the baptism itself but rather what happened after Jesus' baptism when he was praying. Hence, the focus shifts away from the baptism to the divine affirmation and empowerment Jesus receives.

[21] After all the people had been baptized and Jesus also had been baptized and was praying, heaven was opened [22] and the Holy Spirit descended upon him in bodily form like a dove. And a voice came from heaven, "You are my beloved Son; with you I am well pleased."

Luke emphasizes the success of John's preaching by saying that all the people were baptized. The universal theme of salvation prepared in the sight of all, announced by Simeon (2:31), is again underscored.

Luke brings the reader into an intimate moment of Jesus' personal prayer. The depth of his relationship with God is illuminated through the physical symbol of a hovering dove and words of divine affirmation. The motif of Jesus at prayer occurs regularly throughout the Gospels, especially at critical turning points or moments of decision. He prayed in a deserted place when the crowds pressed around him (5:16), on the mountain the night before choosing the Twelve (6:12), in solitude before asking the disciples about his identity (9:18), on the mountain where he was transfigured (9:28–29), in a certain place where he taught his disciples the "Our Father" (11:1–4), on the Mount of Olives during his time of agony (22:39–46), and finally, at the moment of his death (23:46). Through prayer he continually drew strength and inspiration from his relationship with God.

Having already played a prominent part in the unfolding drama of salvation (1:15, 35, 41, 67; 2:25, 26), the Holy Spirit descends upon Jesus here, so that when he is led into the desert he is filled with the Spirit (4:1) and later when in the Nazareth synagogue he can affirm that he is anointed with the Spirit (4:18). Just as Jesus is full of the Holy Spirit, so also he promises the apostles after his resurrection that the Spirit will come upon them making them "witnesses in Jerusalem, throughout Judea and Samaria, and to the ends of the earth" (Acts 1:8).

The voice from heaven cites part of Psalm 2:7, "You are my son," with the addition of "beloved" to qualify the kind of son Jesus is. Through this disclosure the closest kind of familial relationship is affirmed between Jesus and the heavenly speaker. By claiming Jesus as his son, God binds himself to Jesus in the most intimate way possible. For Jesus to be the son of God means that he is to do the will of God faithfully and completely. Divine sonship is not so much a privilege to be enjoyed but a calling to be lived out. Later in his second volume Luke has Paul cite Psalm 2:7 as a scripture fulfilled by Jesus' resurrection (Acts 13:33).

The second part of the divine message in Luke 3:22 alludes to a form of Isaiah 42:1, "my chosen one with whom I am pleased." Highly valuing the chosen one, God is well pleased with Jesus. This revelation underscores Jesus' empowerment by God, an empowerment that is reaffirmed at the transfiguration when the heavenly voice proclaims to the few disciples: "This is my chosen Son; listen to him" (9:35).

Jesus' divine claim by the Holy Spirit is for the purpose of mission, a mission that will be programmatically announced in Nazareth (4:16–19) and that will unfold in the rest of the narrative.

For reflection: Whether a person has been baptized as an infant or an adult there are often rich symbols such as the baptismal candle and robe, along with pictures to remind one of that great event. If a person was baptized as an adult, the pouring of water—or perhaps immersion—and the anointing with oil are also vivid memories. Sometimes, however, a person may look upon one's baptism as a fixed point in time, rather than an ongoing experience to be lived out. Sacramentally it is not correct for a believer to use the past tense and say: "I was baptized." Rather, baptism is to be an ongoing experience of Christian life to be continually embraced in the present. Thus, as a living sacrament a believer is to affirm: "I am baptized," and this means a continual dying to sin, and rising to new life in Christ. Just as Jesus faithfully lived out his baptismal experienced as a son of God, so are believers to embrace dynamically their new identity as sons and daughters of God. How do you live out your baptism in day to day life?

The Temptation in the Desert (4:1–13)

After the heavenly voice identifies Jesus as God's Son, Luke traces his ancestry back to Adam, the son of God (3:23–38). In this genealogy Luke answers two important questions. Who is Jesus? He is God's beloved Son. Where did he come from? From Joseph, "as was thought" (3:23), whose ancestry includes David, which goes back to Abraham, the father of the Jews, and finally to Adam, who stands at the origin of the entire human race. A third question also arises: What kind of person is the son of God? Luke answers this query by narrating Jesus' confrontation with the devil in the wilderness. Jesus is the kind of son whose absolute trust is in God, and hence, faced with a three-fold testing, he is faithfully obedient to God alone.

> 4:1 Filled with the holy Spirit, Jesus returned from the Jordan and was led by the Spirit into the desert 2for forty days, to be tempted by the devil. He ate nothing during those days, and when they were over he was hungry. 3 The devil said to him, "If you are the Son of God, command this stone to become bread." 4Jesus answered him, "It is written, 'One does not live by bread alone.' " 5Then he took him up and showed

him all the kingdoms of the world in a single instant. ⁶ The
devil said to him, "I shall give to you all this power and their
glory; for it has been handed over to me, and I may give it to
whomever I wish. ⁷ All this will be yours, if you worship me."
⁸ Jesus said to him in reply, "It is written:

'You shall worship the Lord, your God,
and him alone shall you serve.' "

⁹ Then he led him to Jerusalem, made him stand on the
parapet of the temple, and said to him, "If you are the Son of
God, throw yourself down from here, ¹⁰ for it is written:

'He will command his angels concerning you,
to guard you,'

¹¹ and:

'With their hands they will support you,
lest you dash your foot against a stone.' "

¹² Jesus said to him in reply, "It also says, 'You shall not put
the Lord, your God, to the test.' " ¹³ When the devil had
finished every temptation, he departed from him for a time.

Responding to the Spirit's initiative, Jesus returned from the
Jordan and is purposefully led into the wilderness for forty days
to be tempted by the devil. Now, apart from all who had been
baptized, Jesus faces in solitude a supreme test of character,
loyalty, and obedience. From a Native American perspective,
Jesus' sojourn in the desert may be interpreted as a kind of
"vision quest," a profound spiritual experience of self-discovery,
purification, and vocational clarification. In counterpoint to
the Spirit who has directed Jesus to the desert, the devil appears
and cleverly devises a threefold trial to subvert Jesus from his
true identity as God's beloved and to reduce him to a minion in
the kingdom of the demonic. The stage is set for a showdown
between the divine and the diabolic.

After the guiding action of the Spirit, the devil plays a sinister
role by challenging a famished Jesus to use his power as the son
of God to satiate his hunger by turning a stone into bread. Jesus'
desert experience recalls the forty-year sojourn of Israel, a

hungry people, whom the Lord tested with affliction and then fed with manna (8:2–3). Citing scripture from Israel's desert journey, Jesus curtly denies the devil's enticing command: "It is written, 'One does not live by bread alone' " (Dt 8:3). Jesus refuses to allow his own hunger to propel him into submitting to a power from the realm of darkness (cf. 1:79).

Defeated once but not to be denied, the devil leads Jesus to a high place and shows him all the kingdoms of the world. Faced with this visionary spectacle Jesus is told that by transferring his allegiance from the realm of light to the realm of darkness he will be given "all this power and their glory." The devil offers Jesus a shortcut to Messianic rule—an option that avoids rejection, suffering, and death—to become the world's most powerful one. Up to this point we have been led to believe that Caesar Augustus is the one with the power to rule the world (2:1), but now a seemingly greater, demonic power has that authority. Jesus is faced with a choice of idolatry before Satan or loyalty to the one true God. Unlike Israel who forgot that it was the Lord who brought them out of the land of Egypt (Dt 6:12), Jesus remembered that God alone is to be worshiped. Thus he replied to the devil with this command put before Israel long ago: "It is written: 'You shall worship the Lord, your God, and him alone shall you serve' " (Dt 6:13). Jesus does not exempt himself from the obedience required of all Israel. In the battle of wits and wills Jesus remains unreservedly loyal to God and refuses to submit to any force hostile to the divine.

To set the stage for the third and final confrontation between two realms, one good and the other evil, the devil leads Jesus to the lofty heights of the Temple, that sacred place where God's glory dwells. In one last desperate attempt the devil purports to speak with the authority of God's own voice by citing two verses from Psalm 91. Tantalizing Jesus, the devil challenges: If you throw yourself down, God's angels will be there to support you "lest you dash your foot against a stone." The tempter is oblivious, however, to the religious spirit of the very psalm quoted for it is addressed to those who put their trust in God as their refuge and fortress. For Jesus to succumb to the devil's proposition would be to deny that trust. Reaffirming his own intimate relationship with God, Jesus silences Satan with one last citation of Deuteronomy: "It also says, 'You shall not put the Lord, your God, to the test' " (Dt 6:16). For a third time Jesus remains truly obedient to God and a faithful minister of God's kingdom.

The narrator alerts us that the devil has now finished "every temptation" and departed for a time. The author of Hebrews also underscores Jesus' own experience with temptation and explains that because he "was tested through what he suffered, he is able to help those who are being tested" (Heb 2:18) and thus has been able "to sympathize with our weaknesses" (Heb 4:15). The next time that Satan re-emerges to attack Jesus and his followers in Luke is during the time of Passover, just before Jesus' death (22:3, 31, 53). In the meantime, Jesus regularly exercises his power over demons by driving them out (4:33–35, 41).

For reflection: The dominant theme of this passage is Jesus' unwavering trust in the Holy One. His faithful obedience to God alone cogently demonstrates what it means to say in the Our Father: "Thy will be done." This passage reminds even the staunchest Christian that power, whether secular, religious, or personal becomes demonic when it is used for domination and self-aggrandizement. To use one's influence to serve self rather than the poor, the captives, and others in need is indeed a form of idolatry. On the other hand, exercising one's power— whether this relates to material resources, social systems or spiritual gifts—in the service of the Gospel is to be a true disciple. The temptation story encourages us, so that with the Spirit's strength we can confront our own demons and overcome any inclination to use power in a way contrary to our calling.

This passage also challenges us to look at modern wildernesses, such as those areas both urban and rural where people on the margins of society struggle to survive. Are you aware of economic practices and political decisions, whether regional, national, or global, that deplete others' lives and exploit the earth's resources for the benefit of the few who dominate by power and privilege? How would you name and address the demonic forces that marginalize, disenfranchise, and dehumanize those in the area where you live? In what ways are you called to be the voice of the Baptist crying out in these wildernesses, and the witness of Jesus confronting the demons you see there?

Jesus Announces his Mission at Nazareth (4:14–30)

In the stories of many healers, teachers, and religious leaders, a time of trial prepares them for their mission. This is certainly the case with Jesus. Having demonstrated his unfailing commitment, the God of the scriptures entrusts Jesus with a vocation defined by a passage from Isaiah. Luke presents this as a programmatic event taking place in the synagogue at Nazareth. In reading the prophetic text, Jesus solemnly proclaims to the townspeople what kind of Messiah he will be. The theme, recurrent throughout Luke Acts, is clearly sounded: the prophet sent by God is accepted, and then rejected by his own people. The initial enthusiastic acceptance of Jesus' prophetic message is followed immediately by a furious rejection of him.

[14] Jesus returned to Galilee in the power of the Spirit, and news of him spread throughout the whole region. [15] He taught in their synagogues and was praised by all.
[16] He came to Nazareth, where he had grown up, and went according to his custom into the synagogue on the sabbath day. He stood up to read [17] and was handed a scroll of the prophet Isaiah. He unrolled the scroll and found the passage where it was written:
[18] "The Spirit of the Lord is upon me,
because he has anointed me to bring glad tidings to the poor.

He has sent me to proclaim liberty to captives
and recovery of sight to the blind,
to let the oppressed go free,
[19] and to proclaim a year acceptable to the Lord."
[20] Rolling up the scroll, he handed it back to the attendant and sat down, and the eyes of all in the synagogue looked intently at him. [21] He said to them, "Today this scripture passage is fulfilled in your hearing." [22] And all spoke highly of him and were amazed at the gracious words that came from his mouth. They also asked, "Isn't this the son of Joseph?" [23] He said to them, "Surely you will quote me this proverb, 'Physician, cure yourself,' and say, 'Do here in your native place the things that we heard were done in Capernaum.'" [24] And he said, "Amen, I say to you, no prophet is accepted in his own native place. [25] Indeed, I tell you, there were many widows in Israel in the days of Elijah when the sky was closed for three and a half years and a severe famine spread over the entire land. [26] It was to none of these that Elijah was sent, but only to a widow in Zarephath in the land of Sidon. [27] Again, there were many lepers in Israel during the time of Elisha the prophet; yet not one of them was cleansed, but only Naaman the Syrian." [28] When the people in the synagogue heard this, they were all filled with fury. [29] They rose up, drove him out of the town, and led him to the brow of the hill on which their town had been built, to hurl him down headlong. [30] But he passed through the midst of them and went away.

The opening verses set the stage geographically by noting that Jesus returns to Galilee and names the enthusiastic response Jesus has received as he journeyed from synagogue to synagogue. Galilee, a region some forty to fifty miles north of Jerusalem and under the control of Herod Antipas (see 9:7–9; 13:31–32; 23:6–12), is the area where Jesus begins his ministry of teaching and preaching the kingdom of God (4:14, 31; 5:17; see 8:26; 17:11; 23:5, 49, 55; 24:6). The disciples, referred to as "Men of Galilee" in Acts 1:11, are later instructed at the empty tomb to remember his teaching in Galilee, namely "that the Son of Man must be handed over to sinners and be crucified, and rise on the third day" (24:7). The rejection of Jesus in this story is ominously foreshadowed by a prior episode also at the Nazareth synagogue when Jesus' hometown acquaintances conspire to bring him to a violent end (4:29).

Jesus returns to Galilee "in the power of the Spirit" (4:14). Already baptized in the Spirit (3:21–22), then led into the desert by the Spirit (4:1), Jesus is now commissioned by the same Spirit (4:18). Jesus derives his power not from himself but from the Spirit. The nuance of the imperfect tense of the Greek verb *edidasken*, translated here "he taught," indicates that Jesus was teaching on a regular basis before coming to the Nazareth synagogue, an activity he continues throughout the Gospel (4:31; 5:3, 17; 6:6; 13:10, 22; 19:47; 20:1, 21; 21:37; 23:5). Luke notes at the outset that Jesus the teacher "was praised by all" (4:15). Later Luke explains this universal positive response when he narrates Jesus' stop at Capernaum, the next Galilean town: "They were astonished at his teaching because he spoke with authority" (4:32). Jesus speaks with authority because he is empowered with the Spirit.

This was not Jesus' first visit to the synagogue. But having been raised in Nazareth (4:16, see 1:26; 2:4, 39, 51), Jesus, like many other Jewish boys, would have worshiped at the synagogue regularly with his parents. Thus it is not surprising that much of Jesus' activity occurs in the synagogue (4:33, 44; 6:6; 13:10), as does that of early Christian preaching (Acts 13:14; 14:1; 17:10,17; 18:4, 26; 19:8). As was typical then, the Law and the Prophets were read from scrolls rather than books. Jesus unrolls the Isaian scroll to the latter part of the prophet and reads aloud.

Luke 4:18–19 is a citation of Isaiah 61:1–2, with the omission of "to heal the brokenhearted" from Isaiah 61:1, and the addition of "setting free the oppressed" from Isaiah 58:6. Citing a passage originally referring to one of the leaders of the early postexilic Isaian school, Jesus applies the words "the Spirit of the Lord is upon me . . . " to himself and thus proclaims that the messianic era has dawned. The anointing of Jesus, already having occurred at his baptism, clearly designates him as the Messiah. The Greek verb *chriō* (meaning "anoint," from which "Christ" derives) is used to translate the Hebrew term for "Messiah." Later Peter confesses that Jesus is the "Messiah of God" (9:20, see 23:35), without understanding that the Messiah must suffer (9:22; 24:26, 46).

The mission of Jesus is "to bring glad tidings to the poor" (4:18). Also translated "to bring good news," this expression is a hallmark of Luke's Gospel (1:19; 4:43; 7:22). The good news is nothing other than the kingdom of God (4:43). Hence, Jesus is the herald of God's kingdom. The term "poor," as well as the words "captives," "blind," and "oppressed," are to be taken literally, although they are not without metaphorical application. Who are the poor? They are first and foremost those who lack adequate material resources for food, shelter, and clothing. They are the marginalized, excluded from human community, the outcast. Throughout the Gospel they are brought to the forefront (see 6:20; 7:22; 14:13, 21; 16:20, 22; 18:22; 19:8; 21:3). Through no choice of their own, the poor are the economically impoverished. They are the oppressed within Israel and without. Just as the prophets Elijah and Elisha were sent to Gentiles in distress (4:25–27), so also Jesus proclaims good news to the poor among the Gentiles, going beyond geographical, cultural, and ethnic boundaries.

Again, who are the poor? Continuing with the word of Isaiah, Jesus names the poor as the captives, the blind, and the oppressed. They are the ones who are welcomed to the dinner in the kingdom in place of the invited guests who are too preoccupied to attend (14:16–24). Literally, captives are prisoners of war; metaphorically, they are those enslaved by debt. As their debts mount, debtors may lose their property and eventually be imprisoned. The captives, as are the oppressed , are promised their freedom, their release (*aphesis*). Luke uses the same Greek word (*aphesis*) elsewhere for "forgiveness of sins" (1:77) and "debts" (11:4). This term also occurs in Deuteronomy 15, a passage calling for the "relaxation of debts" by creditors and manumission of slaves every seven years (Dt 15:1–18). Some commentators suggest that in this passage Jesus is declaring a Jubilee Year (see Lev 25:8–12). The blind receive their sight, literally and metaphorically. By restoring sight (7:21–22; 18:35), Jesus realizes and fulfills what is said about light, healing, and release in Isaiah 42:6–7: "I have set you as . . . a light to the nations, to open the eyes of the blind, to bring out the prisoners from confinement . . . those who live in darkness" (see Is 49:6; 58:8, 10). As one who opens the eyes of the blind, Jesus is indeed a light to the nations. Metaphorically light is a symbol for the dawn of salvation, inaugurated with Jesus' mission. Simeon pronounces that Jesus is "a light for revelation to the Gentiles" (2:32). In him all people "shall see the salvation of God" (3:6), as the Baptist later proclaims. In Acts the Risen One explains Paul and Barnabas' divine commission using light imagery: "I have made you a light to the Gentiles, that you may be an instrument of salvation to the ends of the earth" (Acts 13:47; see Is 49:6). Before King Agrippa, Paul reports that the Lord sent him "to open [the Gentiles'] eyes, that they may turn from darkness to light and from the power of Satan to God, so that they may obtain forgiveness of sins [*aphesis hamartiōn*]" (Acts 26:18). As a light bearer who brings physical sight and salvation, Jesus serves as the model for others called to herald the Gospel.

The oppressed are sent away free, literally "in liberty" (*en aphesei*). They are oppressed by physical and mental disorders understood to be caused by Satan. The Nazareth pericope is framed by two encounters of conflict between Jesus and Satan. In the temptation scene Jesus refuses to submit to demonic enticements (4:1–13); in a Capernaum synagogue he drives out a demonic spirit that renders the afflicted man unclean (4:33–37), and later brings release to a daughter of Abraham similarly bound by Satan (13:10–17; cf. Acts 10:38).

After Jesus finished reading from the scroll, those present "looked intently at him" (4:20), yet as the narrative unfolds

49

their initial admiration (4:22) turns to indignation (4:28), blinding them to the salvation now being fulfilled, especially, among those outside of Israel (4:25–27). His townspeople are enraged because Jesus, whom they know as "the son of Joseph," gives preference not to his own family and villagers as would be expected in Mediterranean society, but to foreigners like the widow of Zarephath in Elijah's time or the Syrian leper Naaman cured by Elisha who are beyond the "in group." In doing this Jesus defines himself as a prophet, for he proclaims: "no prophet is accepted [*dektos*] in his own native place" (4:24). The hostile rejection Jesus experiences from his hometown folks imprisoned by their own ethnocentricity foreshadows the rejection Jesus will experience from his own nation later on. Although Jesus has proclaimed "a year acceptable [*dektos*] to the Lord" (4:19), he himself is not accepted [*dektos*] by those with whom he grew up.

The far-reaching implications of Jesus' proclamation of good news to the poor threatens those who by placing their security in their own ethnic identity claim superiority over outsiders.

For reflection: This passage brings to light the very heart of the Gospel. There are three main themes. First, the call empowering a person for ministry comes not from oneself, but only from the divine Spirit who anoints those called to service. Second, the recipients of the good news are none other than the poor, the imprisoned, the blind, and the captive. If they are not the focus of mission then the vision of the community of believers is blurred. Finally, the mission of evangelists extends beyond those already within the flock and is to embrace those on the outside, even those who have been excluded, for example, by the church community. There is a difference between those who exclude themselves from the circle of believers by actions that are incompatible with the Gospel, and those who have been ostracized because their beliefs and actions threaten ecclesiastical practices that appear to be contrary to the spirit of the Gospel. To name these may mean paying the price of a prophet who is unaccepted—at least for a time—by those religious leaders whose vision is restricted by the "hometown" mentality.

The Call of Simon the Fisherman (5:1–11)

What he has just proclaimed, Jesus begins to carry out. Entering a synagogue in nearby Capernaum, a significant political and economic center where he had already performed newsworthy events (4:23), Jesus cures a man with a spirit of an unclean demon (4:31–37), with the result that "news of him spread everywhere in the surrounding region."

Still in Capernaum Jesus goes to the home of Simon's mother-in-law. The text does not say whether Peter's wife is present at this time, or even if she is still living. In any case, Jesus heals this otherwise nameless woman when he "rebuked the fever." Demonstrating that the cure is effective and instantaneous, she gets up and fulfills her family social obligations. After this, Luke gives a summary statement of all that Jesus did: "At sunset, all who had people sick with various diseases brought them to him. He laid his hands on each of them and cured them" (4:40). The next day the folks from Capernaum, enthralled with Jesus (4:42; cf. 10:15) unlike the hostile crowd from Nazareth, try to keep him from departing, but Jesus solemnly reminds them of his mission: "To the other towns also I must proclaim the good news of the kingdom of God, because for this purpose I have been sent" (4:43).

The mention of Simon's mother-in-law prepares us for a story about Simon himself. Having announced his mission, taught with authority, and performed healing actions, Jesus calls collaborators to join him in carrying out his kingdom activity by following him as an itinerant preacher. Jesus does not work apart from but along with others who respond to the divine call coming through him.

⁵:¹ While the crowd was pressing in on Jesus and listening to the word of God, he was standing by the Lake of

Gennesaret. [2] He saw two boats there alongside the lake; the fishermen had disembarked and were washing their nets.

[3] Getting into one of the boats, the one belonging to Simon, he asked him to put out a short distance from the shore. Then he sat down and taught the crowds from the boat. [4] After he had finished speaking, he said to Simon, "Put out into deep water and lower your nets for a catch." [5] Simon said in reply, "Master, we have worked hard all night and have caught nothing, but at your command I will lower the nets." [6] When they had done this, they caught a great number of fish and their nets were tearing. [7] They signaled to their partners in the other boat to come to help them. They came and filled both boats so that they were in danger of sinking. [8] When Simon Peter saw this, he fell at the knees of Jesus and said, "Depart from me, Lord, for I am a sinful man." [9] For astonishment at the catch of fish they had made seized him and all those with him, [10] and likewise James and John, the sons of Zebedee, who were partners of Simon. Jesus said to Simon, "Do not be afraid; from now on you will be catching men." [11] When they brought their boats to the shore, they left everything and followed him.

Using his sources, primarily the call narrative in Mark 1:16–20 and perhaps the post-resurrection event recounted in John 21:1–11, Luke creatively weaves together three episodes in this engaging story: Jesus' successful teaching on the Lake of Gennesaret (5:1–3), the amazingly bountiful fishing venture (5:4–7), and the call of Simon and his companions who respond positively by leaving all to follow Jesus (5:8–11).

The scene opens with the crowd listening to "the word of God," a praiseworthy activity when it is combined with observance as Jesus later proclaims: "Blessed are those who hear the word of God and observe it" (11:28). The size of the crowd pressing in on Jesus anticipates the "great number of fish" that are later caught (5:6). From this populous scene on the lake, the lens of the story brings into view two boats and then focuses on just one, that belonging to Simon, the main character.

Moving into the midst of a small fishing business Jesus establishes his authority by surprisingly directing those experienced in their trade. Simon responds to Jesus' command to lower the nets by calling him "Master (*epistatēs*)," acknowledging his authority as one who "stands over," the literal meaning of the Greek title (see also Lk 8:24, 45; 9:33, 49). In spite of his reservation, Simon complies with Jesus' command. Like Mary who first wondered (1:34) before submitting to the divine invitation (1:38), Simon raised an objection but then committed himself in faith to Jesus by following his instruction. The use of the plural in 5:5–7 reminds us that Simon's companions are not far from the center of activity, although Simon himself, called Simon Peter in 5:8, remains their spokesperson as he is throughout the Gospel (5:8; 8:45; 9:20, 33; 12:41; 18:28). Peter is also highlighted as the one who witnesses the empty tomb (24:12) and is named as one to whom the Risen Lord appeared (24:34). The abundance of fish caught recalls the large number in John 21:11 where 153 are enumerated.

Peter's response to the over-abundant catch of fish was one of awe-inspired fear, prompting him not only to acknowledge Jesus as Lord, but also to ask him to depart from him, "a sinful man." Like the call story of Isaiah (6:1–8), the revelation of the Holy One leads to an awareness of being unworthy, indeed of being sinful. Peter's own sinfulness in the form of his three-fold denial is recounted later in the Gospel (22:54–65).

Jesus responds to Peter's fear, as well as to the astonishment of James and John, mentioned here for the first time, with the invitation: "Do not be afraid; from now on you will be catching human beings [NAB has 'men']" (5:10). Using the metaphor of fishing, the Lukan Jesus transforms it to say that the Peter and his companions will now be "catching human beings." Continuing with the metaphor, we can say that the bait is the "word of God" (5:1), but, departing from the metaphor, the catching will bring not death but a new way of life. The expression "from now on" underscores this vocation as the beginning of something different, the beginning of a new period of salvation (1:48; 12:52; 22:18, 69).

The response of those called was as radical and complete as it was immediate: "They left everything and followed him" (5:11). With the decision to leave behind their small fishing enterprise, their means of livelihood, Peter and the Zebedee brothers were entrusting their lot with one who had radically changed their lives in one encounter. The total response to follow their Lord and Master was first of all a physical act of going after him. At a deeper level their response was an expression of faithful allegiance to Jesus. The verb "to follow" is often used in the specialized sense of becoming a disciple (5:27–28; 9:23, 49, 57, 59, 61; 18:22, 28, 43; 22:39, 54). The action of giving up one's possession is a radical, symbolic statement of a total response to Jesus, God's prophet (5:28; 14:33; 18:22–23). Although the renunciation of goods does not become the norm for discipleship in Luke, it is one of the most radical actions symbolizing a complete response.

For reflection: The call to discipleship is no less real today for us than it was for the fisherman centuries ago on the Lake of Gennesaret, for the one who calls is indeed the Living One. Although believers throughout the ages may not be impressed by the way they themselves have been called—thinking that it cannot compare to that of Peter or Paul, or to that of Martha or Mary—the invitation has nonetheless been offered. Similar to Peter and his companions, this invitation most often comes in the context of daily life, whether that be driving the kids to school, working as a day-laborer in the fields, dealing with the multiple pressures at the office, doing the laundry at home, or cutting the grass on the weekend. If we are like Peter, and most of us are in some way, it would not be surprising for our initial response to echo his: "Depart from me, Lord, for I am a sinful person." Yet this passage vividly reminds us, that the Master invites those who are not perfect, who have stumbled and fallen, to come follow him.

A Leper is Cleansed and a Paralytic Healed (5:12–26)

[12] Now there was a man full of leprosy in one of the towns where he was; and when he saw Jesus, he fell prostrate, pleaded with him, and said, "Lord, if you wish, you can make me clean." [13] Jesus stretched out his hand, touched him, and said, "I do will it. Be made clean." And the leprosy left him immediately. [14] Then he ordered him not to tell anyone, but "Go, show yourself to the priest and offer for your cleansing what Moses prescribed; that will be proof for them." [15] The report about him spread all the more, and great crowds assembled to listen to him and to be cured of their ailments, [16] but he would withdraw to deserted places to pray.

[17] One day as Jesus was teaching, Pharisees and teachers of the law were sitting there who had come from every village of Galilee and Judea and Jerusalem, and the power of the Lord was with him for healing. [18] And some men brought on a stretcher a man who was paralyzed; they were trying to bring him in and set [him] in his presence. [19] But not finding a way to bring him in because of the crowd, they went up on the roof and lowered him on the stretcher through the tiles into the middle in front of Jesus. [20] When he saw their faith, he said, "As for you, your sins are forgiven." [21] Then the scribes and Pharisees began to ask themselves, "Who is this who speaks blasphemies? Who but God alone can forgive sins?" [22] Jesus knew their thoughts and said to them in reply, "What are you thinking in your hearts? [23] Which is easier, to say, 'Your sins are forgiven,' or to say, 'Rise and walk'? [24] But that you may know that the Son of Man has authority on earth to forgive sins"— he said to the man who was paralyzed, "I say to you, rise, pick up your stretcher, and go home." [25] He stood up immediately before them, picked up what he had been lying on, and went home, glorifying God. [26] Then astonishment seized them all and they glorified God, and, struck with awe, they said, "We have seen incredible things today."

After the call of Simon and his companions, Luke, now closely following the sequence in Mark 1:40–3:6, recounts a series of healings by Jesus that bring him into direct conflict with the religious leaders of his day, the scribes and Pharisees (5:12–6:11). In the first healing (5:12–16), a man "full of leprosy" encounters Jesus in the public arena of the city—the place where Jesus announced that he was sent to proclaim the kingdom God (4:43)—certainly not a welcomed or permissible place for a person with a socially unacceptable condition to be. Probably not to be associated with today's Hansen's disease, biblical leprosy was a disfiguring skin affliction that banishes one to social isolation (Lv 13–14; Nm 5:2–3; 2 Kgs 7:3–9; 15:5). The leper, by falling prostrate, begging, and asserting that Jesus can help him, acknowledges Jesus' authority and superior status. This story thus follows a familiar pattern in healing miracles: an encounter with the healer takes place, the problem is indicated and a compelling request for healing is made.

Jesus responds immediately by stretching out his hand and touching this man. Through personal, physical contact, Jesus crosses the conventional boundary between the clean and the unclean. Rendering himself unclean, Jesus proclaims to the leper: "Be made clean." The result is immediate, as is the case with many of Jesus' healings (4:39; 5:25; 8:44, 55; 13:13; 18:43). Then, after commanding him to silence, Jesus orders the man to show himself to the priest (Lv 14:2–9), thus complying with the Law upheld by the teachers who will challenge Jesus in the next scene (5:17). Jesus' action, authenticated by the priests, makes it possible for this outcast to be re-integrated into society, to go freely into the city, and to participate in the Temple worship of God.

Contrary to Jesus' intention to keep this quiet, the report spread rapidly so that great crowds gather around him to listen to his teaching and certainly to be cured. Surrounded by many who are attracted by the power of his words and deeds, Jesus customarily withdraws to a deserted place to pray (the imperfect tense of the verb "withdraw" suggests repeated action, 5:16). This demonstrates that Jesus' power comes from God, and that Jesus needs to keep in intimate union with God in order to bring God's healing. This also prepares him for the crescendo of opposition that follows.

The story of the paralytic begins as a quest for healing, develops into a serious controversy, and culminates in a positive response that brings physical healing and forgiveness of sins (5:17–26). Ironically, the episode opens with Jesus *teaching* the Pharisees and the *teachers of the law* who were there sitting—a posture of authority. In noting that these religious leaders—mentioned here for the first time in the Gospel—were from "every village of Galilee and Judea and Jerusalem," Luke emphasizes the universal representation of authorities who are around Jesus. This raises the question whether they will receive Jesus' teaching and acknowledge that God's authority is manifest in him? They do neither. Instead they accuse Jesus of blasphemy, thus creating a serious obstacle to the paralytic's quest for healing.

The charge of blasphemy is the second of two obstacles. The first is a physical one. The men who brought the paralytic were prevented by the crowd from bringing him into Jesus' presence, so they ingeniously lowered the man "through the tiles." Changing Mark's account ("opened up the roof," 2:4), Luke notes that they let him down through the tiles, a descriptive phrase designating the house as Greco-Roman, thus reflecting the Hellenistic setting of Luke's Gospel (5:19). Jesus responds positively to them because of "their faith," that is, the faith of the stretcher bearers and the paralytic (5:20).

Used here for the first time in Luke's Gospel, faith implies courageous action, perseverance and trust that God can work through Jesus. In subsequent healings Jesus underscores the importance of faith by asserting: "Your faith has saved you" (7:50; 8:48; 17:19; 18:42). Indeed, faith is the fundamental response of the people to God's visitation (see also 7:9; 8:25; 18:8; 20:5). After acknowledging the faith present, Jesus surprisingly declares to the paralytic: "Your sins have been forgiven to you" (5:20, literal translation; the perfect passive connotes that forgiveness occurs by divine authority), offering healing on a very different level than what was expected.

In making this pronouncement Jesus assumes that forgiveness of sins is integral to healing. This does not imply that health problems are caused by moral failures, but it does suggest that a person's sins are a factor in sickness, a view reflected in the Old Testament (see Ex 20:5; Dt 5:9) and in John's Gospel (9:2). As the religious leaders discuss among themselves his actions, Jesus already knows their ominous thoughts (5:21–22). His foreknowledge recalls Simeon's prophecy that in Mary's child "the thoughts of many hearts may be revealed" (2:35).

Jesus answers his objectors by healing the paralytic and instructing him to pick up his stretcher and go home. Jesus interprets this visible healing action as a external sign of forgiveness, a liberating action not visible to human eyes. The man then responds immediately, and does what Jesus says, "glorifying God" (5:25). All those present, presumably the scribes and Pharisees as well, are astonished; they also glorify God, saying "We have seen incredible things today" (5:26). However, this word of praise soon evaporates, for after two sabbath controversies, they now become "enraged and discussed together what they might do to Jesus" (6:11).

For reflection: As part of my pastoral care work at a large urban medical center I regularly facilitate a "Faith and Life" group on the Behavioral Health Unit. The one hope that most participants regularly identify is that of healing. Many come for treatment on their own accord because they recognize their need to be in a safe place; others are brought there—like the paralytic—by friends, family members, or community health workers because of the crippling mental condition they are in. I often invite the group members to respond to two questions. Recognizing that all of us need to be made whole, I first ask them to name the areas in which they desire healing. Then, I ask them to identify resources, specifically spiritual resources, that they have drawn upon to facilitate healing. Most often, they respond by saying "prayer" and "faith." They say this even though at the time they may feel that it is very hard to pray or that their faith is woefully inadequate. By sharing their own faith—however impoverished it may seem to them—they offer support to each other as well as receive encouragement.

Many times the obstacles to the healing we desire may seem to be far greater than that faced by the paralytic. However, by reaching out to others who believe not for answers—but for their caring presence, we open ourselves to the healing of Jesus that comes through them.

III

Teaching the Disciples
and Sending them on Mission
(6:12–9:50)

The confrontation between Jesus and the scribes and Pharisees over sabbath observance leaves them enraged. In their hostility they plot what they might do to Jesus (6:11). Responding to his rejection by the religious leaders, Jesus selects from among many disciples twelve apostles who will represent reconstituted Israel (6:12–16). Then, Jesus begins to teach his disciples in the Sermon on the Plain about the radical new way of life to which they have been called (6:17–49). Following this instruction he resumes his healing ministry by restoring to health the dying slave of a Roman centurion (7:1–10), and then by raising to life the only son of a widow from Naim (7:11–17).

After being off stage for four chapters, John the Baptist re-emerges with his disciples. John sends two of them to figure out who this Jesus is (7:18–23). And Jesus explains to the crowds who John is (7:24–35). With two groups of disciples, those of Jesus and those of John, the multitude must have been wondering how John fit into the picture. Following the discussion about John, Luke presents a moving story about a nameless woman who responds generously to the warm hospitality and gift of forgiveness she receives from Jesus (7:36–50). Then Luke highlights a group of women who have accompanied Jesus from town to village as he proclaims the good news of the kingdom of God (8:1–3).

Resuming his role as teacher, Jesus tells a large crowd two parables about how the kingdom of God is to be received: the parable of the sower followed by an explanation (8:4–15) and the parable of the lamp (8:16–18). In a brief section Luke focuses his lens on Jesus' new understanding of family beyond biological ties, embracing all "those who hear the word of God and act on it" (8:19–21). Using his power to calm a storm at sea and thus the fears of his troubled disciples, Jesus calls them to task for their inadequate faith (8:22–25).

After two extended healing passages, that of the Gerasene demoniac (8:26–39) and of Jairus' daughter together with the woman with the hemorrhage (8:40–56), Jesus sends the Twelve on a mission to heal (9:1–6). Their success perplexes Herod who recalls how he removed the threat of John's prophetic judgment by beheading him (9:7–9). This literary interlude creates a sense of elapsed time while the Twelve are on mission. After they returned and reported their accomplishments, they had no patience with the large crowd around Jesus. Contrary to their wish to have the crowd dismissed, Jesus took charge of the situation and fed more than five thousand with abundance (9:10–17).

Previously John's disciples had inquired about Jesus' identity; now Jesus himself asks the disciples how he is understood. Neither the crowds nor Peter come close to a full understanding (9:18–21), and so Jesus teaches them about the necessary fate of the Son of Man (9:22, the first passion prediction), and the radical conditions for discipleship (9:23–27). After the somber notes of suffering and death for the Master, in addition to self-denial and the cross for the disciples, Luke follows Mark in narrating the transfiguration of Jesus (9:28–36). A healing story of a boy with a demon (9:37–43a), the reiteration of the passion prediction (9:43b–45), a teaching about the greatest in the kingdom (9:46–48), and an outsider casting out demons (9:49–50), round out this section.

Choosing of the Twelve (6:12–16)

> [12] In those days he departed to the mountain to pray, and he spent the night in prayer to God. [13] When day came, he called his disciples to himself, and from them he chose Twelve, whom he also named apostles: [14] Simon, whom he named Peter, and his brother Andrew, James, John, Philip, Bartholomew, [15] Matthew, Thomas, James the son of Alphaeus, Simon who was called a Zealot, [16] and Judas the son of James, and Judas Iscariot, who became a traitor.

In preparation for selecting twelve apostles from among the disciples, Jesus spends the night in "prayer to God." Regularly in Luke's Gospel Jesus prays before important decisions are made, new directions taken, or an impending crisis encountered (3:21; 5:16; 9:18, 28–29; 22:40–46). In the biblical world, as well as in other religious traditions, a mountain is the place where the spiritual person communes with God. Although Luke does not tell us about the content of Jesus' prayer, he does indicate its duration: it lasted the whole night. This extended period of contemplation prepared Jesus to select individuals who would become trusted representatives. Yet the presence among the Twelve of Judas Iscariot, whom Luke tells us "became a traitor" (6:16; see 22:3–6, 47–48), indicates that not all of them remained faithful to the divine plan.

Previously in Luke Jesus had called three fishermen, Simon, James and John who left everything and followed him (5:1–11); then he called Levi, a tax collector, to follow him (5:27–32), while saying little about what was expected of them. While the selection of the group in 6:12–16 does not spell out their function or purpose, the two collective names, "Twelve," and "apostles," are significant. Clearly recalling the twelve tribes of Israel, the Twelve represent continuity with Israel. As Luke explains later, they "will sit on thrones judging the twelve tribes of Israel" (22:30), thus taking a position of authority over the twelve tribes. What qualifies a person to be among that number?

As Luke clarifies at the beginning of Acts regarding Judas' replacement, "it is necessary that one of the men who accompanied us the whole time the Lord Jesus came and went among us, beginning from the baptism of John until the day on which he was taken up from us, become with us a witness to his resurrection" (Acts 1:21–22).

Jesus named the twelve "apostles," who in Luke are almost always restricted to the Twelve (except for Acts 14:4, 14). In the New Testament apostle is a special term for a Christian emissary, or official representative of the one who sends. A few chapters later Jesus gives the threefold mission of the Twelve: they are to have authority over demons, to heal the sick, and to proclaim the kingdom of God (9:1–2).

The diversity among the group is evident: there are four Galilean fishermen, a zealot, a tax collector (Matthew, probably not the same as Levi), one with a Greek name (Philip), and a traitor. At the head of each New Testament list of the Twelve is Peter (Mt 10:2–4; Mk 3:16–19; Lk 6:14–16; Acts 1:13), a name from the Greek *petra*, meaning rock. The first four consist of two sets of brothers: Peter and Andrew, and James and John. Three of these, Peter, James and John, are a select subgroup who are present at the raising of Jairus' daughter (8:51) and the transfiguration (9:28). James and John are not timid, for they will implore Jesus to call down fire from heaven to consume the inhospitable Samaritans (9:54). Those in the later two groups of four, with the exception of Judas Iscariot, are hardly mentioned in the rest of the New Testament or in the early Christian tradition.

For reflection: Given Luke's restrictive understanding of apostle mentioned above, most Christians today would probably not call themselves by this title. Nonetheless, this passage remains instructive. Through the divine plan of God the followers of Jesus are called by name to witness to the saving deeds of Jesus and hence to advance the kingdom of God. Like the name Peter, some find in their birth name special meaning, or may have taken a saint's name at Confirmation whose virtuous life stands out as a shining example of the Christian way.

Beyond this, those in ministry may discover through prayer a special identity, or "name," that is rooted in their relationship with Christ. The prophetic author of Revelation solemnly announces this naming using the imagery of a white amulet: "Whoever has ears ought to hear what the Spirit is saying to the churches. . . . I shall also give a white amulet upon which is inscribed a new name, which no one knows except the one who receives it" (Rv 2:17). In the context of this passage, the name is probably that of the risen and glorified Jesus. The "new name" for the disciple can take various forms whether that be "Proclaimer of the Word," "Encourager," or "Wounded Healer"—an expression from Henri Nouwen. What name best describes your calling as a baptized believer?

Beatitudes and Woes (6:17–26)

¹⁷And he came down with them and stood on a stretch of level ground. A great crowd of his disciples and a large number of the people from all Judea and Jerusalem and the coastal region of Tyre and Sidon ¹⁸came to hear him and to be healed of their diseases; and even those who were tormented by unclean spirits were cured. ¹⁹Everyone in the crowd sought to touch him because power came forth from him and healed them all.
²⁰And raising his eyes toward his disciples he said:
"Blessed are you who are poor,
for the kingdom of God is yours.
²¹Blessed are you who are now hungry,
for you will be satisfied.
Blessed are you who are now weeping,
for you will laugh.
²²Blessed are you when people hate you,
and when they exclude and insult you,

and denounce your name as evil on account of the Son
of Man.
23 Rejoice and leap for joy on that day! Behold, your
reward will be great in heaven. For their ancestors
treated the prophets in the same way.
24 But woe to you who are rich,
for you have received your consolation.
25 But woe to you who are filled now,
for you will be hungry.
Woe to you who laugh now,
for you will grieve and weep.
26 Woe to you when all speak well of you,
for their ancestors treated the false prophets in this way."

In selecting the twelve apostles Jesus has symbolically gathered a renewed Israel. Now he instructs all those assembled
about the radical new way of life in God's kingdom. Jesus
emphatically states the norms of behavior and the status before
God of those who are on the opposite ends of the social and
economic spectrum. In contrast to Matthew who has nine beatitudes formulated in the third person, Luke has four beatitudes
and four woes addressed in the second person. To each of the
Lukan beatitudes there is a sharply contrasted judgment of woe.

For whom is Jesus' teaching intended? The narrator clearly
directs our attention to the great crowd of disciples (6:17). And
in a subtle yet dramatic gesture Jesus begins to speak by "raising
his eyes toward his disciples" (6:20). However, they are not the
only ones present. There is also a "large number of the people"
from a wide geographical area. Those from "all Judea and Jerusalem" (6:17) represent the people Israel; and those from "the
coastal region of Tyre and Sidon," represent the Gentiles. Jesus'
message is universal, addressing all those who seek the kingdom
as well as those who are in danger of rejecting it.

Many in the days of Jesus as well as in our own long to hear a
message that will bring us a far deeper level of joy than we have
yet known. That joy is to be found by embracing the fullness of
God's reign, as expressed in the beatitudes.

The first beatitude, "Blessed are you who are poor," fulfills the good news Jesus announced at Nazareth when he proclaimed "glad tidings to the poor" (4:18). Who are the poor? Unlike in Matthew's version where the poor are spiritualized: "Blessed are the poor in spirit . . . " (Mt 5:3), in Luke the poor are the materially destitute, the hungry, and the weeping. Both economically deprived and socially marginalized, the poor are those without dignity, honor, or respect in society. Lacking any power of their own, they are unable to alter their status.

In a dramatic reversal of fortunes, Jesus proclaims that the poor are "blessed" not because of the miserable condition in which they find themselves. Jesus does not glorify poverty, a condition that often leads to premature death. In our own time Dorothy Day reminds us that living in poverty is hardly a condition to be romanticized. The poor are not "blessed" because of any prior conversion experience, attained virtue, or interior disposition. Nor are they proclaimed blessed because of the good deeds they might have accumulated or fidelity to the covenant they have shown. The poor are "blessed" for one reason only, and that is because "Yours is the kingdom of God." By speaking directly to them using the second person plural Jesus, the kingdom preacher, establishes an intimate connection with God's chosen ones. God's reign is for you poor, yes, particularly for you! And it is yours already now! They do not have to wait for it until some distant future.

Now is the time of grace for the poor. In the beatitudes Jesus emphasizes God's new initiative, the free gift of grace. Jesus reveals and proclaims the breakthrough of divine mercy. God's favor is always present before any human action.

Later in the Gospel one of the criminals clinging to life as he hangs on the cross next to Jesus cries out in faith: "Jesus, remember me when you come into your kingdom" (23:42). Hearing his plea, Jesus welcomes him into the kingdom that very day, saying: "Today you will be with me in Paradise" (23:43). Those who embrace God's beloved son by entering into a close personal relationship with him experience already now the blessing of God's presence.

The fourth beatitude addresses those who are hated, excluded, insulted and denounced because of their relationship to the "son of humanity" (the meaning of Son of Man). They are promised a day when they will rejoice and leap for joy. As Jesus tells them, "Your reward will be great in heaven." In Luke God's pattern is one of rejection and acceptance. Although Jesus, God's prophet, is rejected by the leaders of the people, like the prophets of old, he is accepted and embraced by God as the beloved son (3:22; 9:35). Similarly, those who are rejected by evildoers because of their fidelity to Jesus are embraced by God. Confronted with debilitating adversity, the disciples are sustained by their unwavering commitment to God's reign.

Those who oppose the kingdom are directly addressed in the series of four woes. Recalling prophetic oracles from the Jewish scriptures, the woes are pronouncements that serve as strong warnings to the rich, to those with filled stomachs, to those who make merry, and finally to those who are well acclaimed by others. These four descriptions can easily refer to one group.

Who are the rich? These are the ones who exercise power, receive honor, and possess many things. Enjoying these privileges, they are the ones who do not commit themselves to Jesus as his disciples, and hence they do not embrace the kingdom he proclaims. The rich are under divine judgment because they have had it good in this life, and have turned a deaf ear to Jesus' message or to the pleas of the poor. The rich would probably be those who do not give when they are asked (6:30), those who lend money expecting repayment (6:34), those who build larger storage barns to horde their possessions (12:16–21), and those who fail to see people like the poor Lazarus lying at their door (16:19–31).

Jesus does not ostracize the rich nor does he say that there is not hope for them. As the rest of the Gospel story unfolds, we hear that Jesus is the guest of those well enough off to host a banquet, and that he invites himself to dine with Zacchaeus, a wealthy tax collector. The invitation to repentance and discipleship is offered to the wealthy who are called to share their possessions by giving alms (12:33), by selling all they have and giving to the poor (18:18–23), or by making their resources available for the needs of the community (Acts 2:45; 4:32).

For reflection: The good news of the beatitudes is the comfort they offer to the destitute. Consolation comes not in the form of empty promises, but as a welcome into the community of God where love, justice and harmony are established. Jesus has promised the poor that the kingdom of God is theirs now, and it is the task of all contemporary Christians to help bring this about. There are increasing rather than decreasing numbers of poor throughout the world today who experience overwhelming oppression. To these poor the reality of God's reign may seem as distant as the farthest planet. Do they also not long to experience the love of God, not just as an inner awareness of the living God, but also as a genuine ongoing response of Christians to their needs?

Who are the poor in our midst—the non-persons, the in-significant ones in both church and society? Do we hear the cry of the poor and stand in solidarity with them? In responding to their needs, do we allow our own hearts to be converted from a sense of self-sufficiency to total dependence on God's love?

Love of Enemies (6:27–36)

[27] "But to you who hear I say, love your enemies, do good to those who hate you, [28] bless those who curse you, pray for those who mistreat you. [29] To the person who strikes you on one cheek, offer the other one as well, and from the person who takes your cloak, do not withhold even your tunic. [30] Give to everyone who asks of you, and from the one who takes what is yours do not demand it back. [31] Do to others as you would have them do to you. [32] For if you love those who

love you, what credit is that to you? Even sinners love those who love them. [33] And if you do good to those who do good to you, what credit is that to you? Even sinners do the same. [34] If you lend money to those from whom you expect repayment, what credit [is] that to you? Even sinners lend to sinners, and get back the same amount. [35] But rather, love your enemies and do good to them, and lend expecting nothing back; then your reward will be great and you will be children of the Most High, for he himself is kind to the ungrateful and the wicked. [36] Be merciful, just as [also] your Father is merciful.

Addressing the same crowd of disciples and people who heard the beatitudes and woes with the words "you who hear," Jesus solemnly teaches about the radical demand of the law of love. Jesus commands: "Love your enemies," and then explains this central theme by giving three specific instructions: "Do good to those who hate you, bless those who curse you, pray for those who mistreat you." In the fourth beatitude the disciples who experienced such negative treatment were called "blessed." Now, Jesus instructs them to develop an attitude of love toward their persecutors expressed in both action ("do good") and speech ("bless," "pray for").

Who were the enemies in the world of Jesus, the disciples, and Luke's community? Jesus' enemies would include those in the synagogue at Nazareth who were "filled with fury" (4:28), his own religious leaders, the scribes and Pharisees, who "became enraged" when he healed on the sabbath (6:11), those who handed him over to death and had him crucified (23:18–25), and those who considered him cursed for being crucified (Gal 3:10,13; 1 Cor 12:3). For the disciples the enemies would be groups such as the Samaritans (9:51–56; 10:25–37; 17:11–17; Acts 8:4–25). The enemies of the Christian community addressed by Luke's Gospel would comprise those synagogue leaders, patrons, family members, and former friends who would have excluded and denounced followers of the Way. Also to be mentioned are the national enemies, the

Romans, who were generally hostile to this new religious movement. These are the enemies Jesus calls his disciples to love, and that means to act well toward them, to bless them, and to pray for them.

The next four counsels in this passage (vv. 29–30) are even more radical in their demand: offer the other cheek, give away even one's undergarment (tunic) when asked, give to everyone who asks, and do not demand back what has been taken. Here Jesus uses forceful and imaginative language that is not necessarily to be taken at face value. On the other hand, taken literally, the counsels to turn the other cheek or to strip oneself naked may possibly cause an aggressor or requestor to take a second look at the victim / giver, a look that could lead to a change in behavior. The requirement to give "to everyone," a Lukan emphasis (contrast Mt 5:42), underscores the universal and non-discriminatory character of the act of giving. Just as radical is the instruction not to demand return of one's possessions when these have been taken. Clearly these instructions are meant to challenge the ordinary ruts in which people think and move.

At the heart of this passage is the Golden Rule, enunciating the principle of reciprocity (v. 31). Jesus radicalizes this norm by giving three examples in the form of conditional questions. He asks: What credit (literally, "grace," "gift") is there in loving, doing good, or lending to those who are in a position to reciprocate? The cultural norm would be to expect repayment—tit for tat. The disciple is to go beyond the practice of reciprocity and thus to transcend self-interest as the motivating principle in relating to others. Jesus implies that there is a higher example to follow, and that is the way of God, mentioned a few verses later.

The Lukan Jesus concludes this section by recapitulating the command to love one's enemies, by stating the reward to be expected, and finally by offering God's action as the model to be imitated. The reward, and motivation as well, for disciples who follow the high standard of excellence offered by Jesus is to become "children of the Most High" (v. 35). If one were to

70

protest, why should I love my enemy and do good to them, Jesus next words become particularly appropriate. The reason is this: that is the way God is. For God "is kind to the ungrateful and the wicked." The disciple is to do as God does. To act in this way is to emulate the mercy of God. Just as God does not choose selectively who is to receive divine kindness, nor should the children of the Most High.

For reflection: The demanding counsels in this passage create a clear imprint of the radical nature of Christianity. To engage the challenging command to love one's enemies, we the readers would do well to name our enemies. Who might these be? Those who have treated us unfairly, those who have discriminated against us? Those who have distorted our good intentions? If we do not make it our aim to love our enemies, then it becomes easy to dismiss or even to hate them. That allows tyranny to reign in our hearts. From a self-interest perspective a person who is consumed by hate pays a high price: the sacrifice of one's own peace of mind and even one's physical well being. The challenge is to acknowledge the hurt that we have experienced from our enemies, and then to let go of any desires for revenge or retaliation. By asking God to help us follow this path we may steer clear of the path of hate.

Over the past ten years I have been privileged to know well David Faber, a Holocaust survivor. Regularly I invite him to speak to the college students in my religious studies courses. As a young teenager David witnessed the torture and death of his brother in Poland. A day later, while hiding with the rest of his family in an abandoned warehouse, he alone survived the bullets of Nazi soldiers who broke into their refuge. After working through his feelings of bitterness, grief and hate, David passionately tells the students: "We have to stop hating one another." And, "there is too much hate in this world." His message is one of tolerance. Hopefully, he is being heard.

When we have difficulty loving our enemies, it may help to remember that like us our enemies are also created in the image and likeness of God, and therefore are worthy of love and respect. Jesus does not say that we have to like our "enemies," but he does call us to love them. In no way are we asked to excuse harmful actions or evil deeds of others. If it is appropriate we may choose to challenge unacceptable behaviors directly. We can always practice "love of enemies" by holding them in prayer before God, as Jesus counsels: "Pray for those who mistreat you."

One final thought. There are those who may consider us their enemy. Bringing into play the Golden Rule, "Do to others as you would have them do to you," we would probably expect that our enemies find a way to love us. As this happens we can become all the more confirmed in our intention to love them.

The Healing of a Centurion's Slave (7:1–10)

In the first two healing stories of chapter 7, the centurion's slave (7:1–10) and the widow's only son (7:11–17), Jesus acts as a great prophet (v. 26). He continues the healing tradition of the prophets of old. There is a striking parallel between the Nazareth passage (4:25–27) and Jesus' healing action in Capernaum and Naim (7:1–17). At the synagogue in Nazareth Jesus refers to the prophet Elijah who brought back to life the widow's son (4:25–26; cf. 1 Kgs 17:1–24), and then to the prophet Elisha who cured Naaman the Syrian army commander (4:27; cf. 2 Kgs 5:1–14). In chapter 7, in inverse order, Luke shows the prophetic action of Jesus when he heals the centurion's slave and then resuscitates the widow's son. Witnesses of this latter event could then truly exclaim: "A great prophet has arisen in our midst," for indeed, "God has visited his people."

[7:1] When he had finished all his words to the people, he entered Capernaum. [2] A centurion there had a slave who was ill and about to die, and he was valuable to him. [3] When he heard about Jesus, he sent elders of the Jews to him, asking him to come and save the life of his slave. [4] They approached

Jesus and strongly urged him to come, saying, "He deserves to have you do this for him, [5]for he loves our nation and he built the synagogue for us." [6]And Jesus went with them, but when he was only a short distance from the house, the centurion sent friends to tell him, "Lord, do not trouble yourself, for I am not worthy to have you enter under my roof. [7]Therefore, I did not consider myself worthy to come to you; but say the word and let my servant be healed. [8]For I too am a person subject to authority, with soldiers subject to me. And I say to one, 'Go,' and he goes; and to another, 'Come here,' and he comes; and to my slave, 'Do this,' and he does it." [9]When Jesus heard this he was amazed at him and, turning, said to the crowd following him, "I tell you, not even in Israel have I found such faith." [10]When the messengers returned to the house, they found the slave in good health.

In this story the centurion sends two delegations to Jesus seeking a benefit. To understand the dynamics involved, it is helpful to consider the significance that the patron–client relationship played in the ancient Mediterranean world. A patron is a social superior, a person in a position of power and authority, and thus was able to benefit clients, who were of inferior status. The centurion was in both roles: on the one hand he was "a person subject to authority," and on the other hand, as a high government official, he had soldiers subject to him (v. 8). In this position he represented Rome to the local population and served as a broker of imperial privileges.

Now the centurion himself was in need, for one of his valued slaves "was ill and about to die" (v. 2). Evidently aware of a Jewish healer in the region, this Gentile sent "elders of the Jews," his clients, to Jesus to ask him "to come and save the life of his slave" (v. 3). These representatives, perhaps synagogue leaders, pleaded his case. They emphasized the worthiness of their patron's request, by praising him: he "loves our nation," a love demonstrated when "he built the synagogue for us" (v. 5). In debt to him, the delegation pressured Jesus for a favorable response. Thus, the centurion related to Jesus as his patron who could mediate God's power by healing his esteemed servant.

Jesus complies and starts out toward his house. Perhaps recognizing that a Jew would violate a rule of purity by entering the home of a Gentile, the centurion sends a second delegation, this time some "friends," with an extended message that unveils his humility. Referring to Jesus as "Lord," the centurion says to him through his representative: "I did not consider myself worthy to come to you; but say the word and let my servant be healed" (v. 7). The one acclaimed to be deserving now lays aside his honor and presents himself as unworthy. Recognizing Jesus' power over death, he asks him to use his healing power.

Hearing about the character of this centurion, Jesus is astonished. Such a response is surprising, since it is usually the crowds who are amazed at what Jesus says and does. Nonetheless, Jesus commends the centurion to the crowds with the words: "I tell you, not even in Israel have I found such faith" (v. 9). Jesus declares this seeker to be worthy, not on the basis of his power, status, financial resources, or even his good deeds, but simply because of his faith. Thus, Jesus praises him as a model for others. This passage does not begin the mission to the Gentiles for it is not yet time, but it does anticipate it. In Acts the Cornelius and Peter episode (Acts 10), a parallel to this passage, powerfully demonstrates how the good news extends to the nations.

For reflection: The main theme here is that God's salvation offered through Jesus extends beyond the people of Israel, even to the enemy. The centurion represents the domination of the occupying power. Yet, Jesus responds favorably to him because of his faith. The command to "love your enemies" (6:27, 35) is demonstrated on a double level in this passage. First, the Roman commander shows his concern for the subjects of the land by building a synagogue for them. Whether this was an expression of his own self-interest—expecting something in return for this benefit (see 6:32–34)—we do not know. Second,

Jesus showed his love for a Roman, considered by his fellow Jews to be the enemy. In a concrete way Jesus models what it means to "love your enemies."

The centurion is a model of faith in Jesus for all. He was able to accept God's prophet, recognizing that all healing comes from him. Not only that, but as one who benefitted the Jewish people, he is a model of someone who loves his enemies. His words "Lord, I am not worthy, but only say the word," have been included in the Eucharistic liturgy, and give courage to all who approach the altar, especially those who may be struggling with a troubled conscience. It is because of God's invitation to partake in the banquet of his Son that we are deemed worthy.

How might faith in the God of Jesus Christ be expressed by those who are not members of the church? Persons in authority, whether this be politically, economically, or in the business world, may themselves have a vibrant relationship with God. Do we recognize this, or do we dismiss them as being on the side of "the enemy"? Are we able to see with our own eyes of faith, how God may be acting in their lives?

Pardon of a Sinful Woman (7:36–50)

The landscape of Jesus' ministry is becoming clearer. He testifies to the disciples of the Baptist that he brings healing to the blind, the lame, the lepers, and the deaf. And he raises the dead (7:22). These powerful actions demonstrate to all the meaning of his mission to bring good news to the poor (4:18; 6:20; 7:22). Sent to bring wholeness, Jesus creates division among the people by reason of their response to his saving deeds. Jesus is rightly accused of being "a friend of tax collectors and sinners" (7:34), yet they are the ones who acknowledge "the righteousness of God" (7:29). Others from the religious elite such as the "Pharisees and scholars of the law", reject "the plan of God for themselves" (7:30), and accuse Jesus of being "a glutton and drunkard" (7:34). In the story of a banquet feast the acceptance and rejection of God's prophet is demonstrated by the responses to Jesus of an uninvited woman and Simon the Pharisee.

³⁶ A Pharisee invited him to dine with him, and he entered the Pharisee's house and reclined at table. ³⁷ Now there was a sinful woman in the city who learned that he was at table in the house of the Pharisee. Bringing an alabaster flask of ointment, ³⁸ she stood behind him at his feet weeping and began to bathe his feet with her tears. Then she wiped them with her hair, kissed them, and anointed them with the ointment. ³⁹ When the Pharisee who had invited him saw this he said to himself, "If this man were a prophet, he would know who and what sort of woman this is who is touching him, that she is a sinner." ⁴⁰ Jesus said to him in reply, "Simon, I have something to say to you." "Tell me, teacher," he said. ⁴¹ "Two people were in debt to a certain creditor; one owed five hundred days' wages and the other owed fifty. ⁴² Since they were unable to repay the debt, he forgave it for both. Which of them will love him more?" ⁴³ Simon said in reply, "The one, I suppose, whose larger debt was forgiven." He said to him, "You have judged rightly." ⁴⁴ Then he turned to the woman and said to Simon, "Do you see this woman? When I entered your house, you did not give me water for my feet, but she has bathed them with her tears and wiped them with her hair. ⁴⁵ You did not give me a kiss, but she has not ceased kissing my feet since the time I entered. ⁴⁶ You did not anoint my head with oil, but she anointed my feet with ointment. ⁴⁷ So I tell you, her many sins have been forgiven; hence, she has shown great love. But the one to whom little is forgiven, loves little." ⁴⁸ He said to her, "Your sins are forgiven." ⁴⁹ The others at table said to themselves, "Who is this who even forgives sins?" ⁵⁰ But he said to the woman, "Your faith has saved you; go in peace."

The story begins with Simon, a Pharisee, inviting Jesus to his home for a banquet. Left untold is why Simon asked Jesus to dine with him. Was he open to learning from this teacher (7:40) or did he want to scrutinize what kind of prophet he was? Whatever his intent, Simon gets the opportunity to do both. Immediately after the setting is introduced with Jesus reclining at table—meaning that he is lying on his side, Hellenistic fashion, with his feet pointing away from the table—an unwelcome woman known to be a sinner intrudes into the banquet scene with an alabaster flask of ointment. In silence she relates to Jesus with dramatic, rather intimate gestures, bathing his feet with her tears (did she enter the home in tears?), then drying them with her hair, kissing and anointing them. The Pharisee is shocked by such impropriety.

With a prophetic awareness of Simon's thoughts, Jesus initiates a dialogue with him, first telling him a parable and then drawing out its implications in Socratic fashion. The parable is clear and straightforward. A creditor forgives the debts of two people, one of whom owed twice as much as the other. Jesus then asks Simon: "Which of them will love him more?" After he answers correctly, Jesus commends him for his insight. Then, asking his host "Do you see this woman?", Jesus contrasts in three poignant statements Simon's cool, inhospitable reception of him with the nameless woman's effusive outpouring of love and devotion.

With the others at table listening, Jesus clearly interprets what the Pharisee has been unable to see (an implied irony, see vv. 39, 44): "So I tell you, her many sins have been forgiven; hence, she has shown great love" (v. 47a). What does Jesus mean by this statement and the following explanation: "But the one to whom little is forgiven, loves little" (v. 47b). Two interpretations are possible: "her many sins were forgiven as a result of her great love," or "her actions of great love manifest her state of forgiveness." Jesus' explanatory comment about "forgiveness of little" leading to "little love" prompts us to conclude that only the second interpretation is possible. This woman has been able to love much because she has already been forgiven much. But why then does Jesus say to her: "Your sins are forgiven"? This can be taken as a pastoral reassurance of her spiritual condition, a reassurance she may have needed in the face of the disapproving eyes of Simon and his guests.

Does the comment about little love imply that for Simon little is forgiven? Perhaps so. However, we are not told how Simon ultimately responds to Jesus who teaches through the parable or to the woman who teaches by her actions. The open ended nature of this story (see also 18:18–23) may be Luke's way of saying to those in his community hesitant to embrace Jesus as God's prophet that there is still time to welcome the salvation offered.

The guests at the banquet speak for the first time at the end of the story, asking "Who is this who even forgives sins?" Later others will similarly inquire about Jesus as they grapple with his identity (8:25; 9:9, 18). Who is Jesus? This will soon be revealed more clearly, though still not understood, in the unfolding narrative (9:20, 22, 35, 44–45; 18:31–34).

In his last pastoral word to the woman, Jesus declares: "Your faith has saved you; go in peace" (7:50). For the first time in Luke's Gospel, faith is joined to salvation (see also 8:12, 48; 17:19; 18:42; Acts 15:11). The healing this woman receives enables her to go in peace, a theme already announced in Zechariah's canticle (1:77,79).

Unraveling a mistaken identity: The woman in this story is unnamed, as is the woman at Bethany in Mark 14:3 and Matthew 26:7. In the anointing story of John 12:1–8 we hear about two sisters, Mary and Martha, who gave a dinner for Jesus. This Mary anointed the feet of Jesus with "a costly perfumed oil" (v. 3). Nothing is said about her being a sinner. However in church tradition since the sixth century the unnamed sinful woman in Luke's story has been associated with the Mary of Bethany (Jn 12:1–8) and even with Mary of Magdalene "from whom seven demons had gone out" (Lk 8:2). This has resulted in a distorted image of Mary Magdalene as one "possessed" and assumed to have been a publicly known sinner, usually associated with the sex trade (and therefore thought to be possessed). Since there is no basis for the conflation of these New Testament texts, the unnamed woman in Luke 7:37 is not to be confused with the two sisters in John 12:1–8, and Mary Magdalene is not to be depicted as a public sinner, but rather is to be honored for being a disciple of the resurrection (Lk 24:10).

For reflection: The theme of this passage is the intimate connection between the experience of forgiveness and the outpouring of love that follows. Two lessons are brought to light. The first is for disciples and would-be disciples of Jesus to embrace the fulness of God's pardon for misdeeds of the past. God's mercy is always there before anyone asks. For many the struggle is not so much to accept God's forgiveness, but to forgive oneself. This means to humbly acknowledge sinful actions, to make amends where possible and to embrace God's healing that comes through Jesus.

Jesus does not chastise the nameless woman in Luke 7, nor does he ever hint that she berate herself for her moral failings. Instead he welcomes her presence, receives the intimate expressions of her love, reassures her of the forgiveness she has already been granted and then sends her on her way in peace. Through his healing words and actions Jesus proclaims the reign of God to those who would receive it.

A second lesson is that out of forgiveness flows love. God's mercy frees those burdened down by sin, heals those suffering from low self-esteem, and restores all to the community of disciples. In this way God empowers us to become "wounded healers," to use Henri Nouwen's famous image, as we extend ourselves in loving service to one another.

Galilean Women Follow Jesus (8:1–3)

8:1 Afterward he journeyed from one town and village to another, preaching and proclaiming the good news of the kingdom of God. Accompanying him were the Twelve 2 and some women who had been cured of evil spirits and infirmities, Mary, called Magdalene, from whom seven demons had gone out, ³ Joanna, the wife of Herod's steward Chuza, Susanna, and many others who provided for them out of their resources.

Luke sets the scene for the Parable of the Sower (8:4–15) by portraying Jesus for the third time as preaching and proclaiming the good news (8:1; see 4:18, 43–44). Accompanying the itinerant Jesus are two groups, the Twelve (6:13–16) and a group of women, three of whom are named. The other Gospels name Galilean women only in connection with the crucifixion and resurrection of Jesus. Luke's concern here is to present Galileans, both men and women, as witnessing to Jesus' teaching and preaching.

Three among the band of women are named: Mary from Magdala, a small Galilean town, Joanna, the wife of Herod's administrator Chuza, and Susanna, who is not further identified or mentioned elsewhere in the Gospels. What these women have in common is that they have been "cured of evil spirits and infirmities" (8:2). Mary's healing is described in more detail; from her seven demons (a perfect number) have been driven out. We are not told why these women chose to follow Jesus. Very probably it is because they, like the Twelve, were called by Jesus to accompany him.

What is highly unconventional, even scandalous, is that these women, at least one of whom was married, were in public as traveling companions of a male itinerant preacher. Normally, the role of women was to manage and work within the household, while the men were expected to handle public matters outside the home. Apart from the home a woman was not to be seen in the presence of a man unless accompanied by a male from her family. This is why in John's Gospel the disciples of Jesus were amazed that he was interacting with a Samaritan woman at Jacob's well (Jn 4:27).

What was the role of these independent-minded women among this mixed group of travelers? The NAB reads: the women "provided for them out of their resources" (8:3). "Provided for" translates the Greek verb *diakoneō*, which literally means to serve, to wait on, to care for. The meaning of this verb in the New Testament ranges from serving at table to serving in a ministerial capacity. The service these women gave may well have been to offer financial or material support. Certainly, Joanna, the wife of Herod's manager, would have had the monetary resources to do so, but this does not mean that all the women in this group were affluent. A second interpretation is that this traveling band of women served Jesus according to their abilities. See Mark 14:8 where it is said that the woman who anointed Jesus had "done what she could."

Whatever their manner of serving Jesus and the Twelve, these women are to be included among the disciples whenever this term is mentioned in the rest of the Gospel. Notice that women from Galilee are specifically mentioned again, though not named individually, at the crucifixion (23:49) and burial of Jesus (23:55). As witnesses of the resurrection, Mary Magdalene and Joanna are named as the ones who announced to the disbelieving disciples that Jesus was alive (24:10, 22). The Galilean women are also probably to be included with Mary, the mother of Jesus, and the Eleven who are gathered in Jerusalem awaiting the Holy Spirit (Acts 1:13–14).

Recent studies have shown that while Luke does give more prominence to women than the other evangelists do, he mainly presents them in a conventional way. Still, there are those who emerge as leaders, such as heads of house churches. Lydia would be one example (Acts 16:14–15, 40).

For reflection: For the past two to three decades the role of women has been discussed and debated in many Christian denominations. For example, for some time the Episcopal church has ordained women priests and others such as Methodists and Presbyterians have ordained female pastors. In the Roman Catholic church women have been given prominent leadership roles as diocesan officials, although the current teaching from Rome is that they cannot be considered as candidates for priesthood. While the Vatican mandates that the ordination of women is not to be discussed, many, including a number of bishops, do not believe that the issue will so easily be resolved.

To raise this question is to not overlook the significant role that women have played in the church. Among the many throughout the centuries there is Catherine of Siena (1347-1380), a lay woman and doctor of the church, a woman known for her life of prayer, courage and sacrifice. In the past century among the numerous exemplary women are Dorothy Day, the co-founder of the Catholic Worker movement, Mother Teresa, the founder of the Sisters of Charity, and Chiara Lubich, the founder of the Focolare Movement. Who are the women in your parish, diocese, and region exercising leadership in the service of the church?

On the other hand there are those in the believing community who have been excluded, dismissed, ridiculed, ignored or silenced because they are female. What forces in the church have kept women from exercising to the fullest their gifts and talents? From your perspective, what charisms have women received and how are these to be exercised in the church today?

Jairus' Daughter and the Woman with a Hemorrhage (8:40–56)

After the accompanying women are introduced in 8:1–3, Luke generally follows his Markan source for the rest of chapter 8. Large crowds journey to Jesus as he teaches them in parables, that of the sower (8:4–8, 11–15) and of the lamp (8:16–18). Jesus' preaching to them is clear: hear the word of God and put it into action. They are to be like the seed on good soil: "They are the ones who, when they have heard the word, embrace it with a generous and good heart, and bear fruit through perseverance" (8:15). To emphasize this point, Jesus redefines the meaning of his biological mother and brothers in terms of the family of disciples, saying: "My mother and my brothers are those who hear the word of God and act on it" (8:21).

Going from land to sea, Jesus demonstrates his power over the winds and sea—the abode of the demons—and then asks his frightened disciples: "Where is your faith?" (8:25). Jesus then sails to Gentile territory on the other side of the lake from Galilee, where he manifests his power over the demons expelling them from a man they had tormented. Having freed him from his isolation among the tombs, Jesus said "return home and recount what God has done for you." Though not called an apostle he became one, proclaiming "throughout the whole town what Jesus had done for him" (8:39). Jesus then sailed back across the lake where his compassionate presence brought healing and new life to two women of faith, one a twelve-year-old and the other an adult who had been hemorrhaging for twelve years.

⁴⁰When Jesus returned, the crowd welcomed him, for they were all waiting for him. ⁴¹And a man named Jairus, an official of the synagogue, came forward. He fell at the feet of Jesus and begged him to come to his house, ⁴²because he had an only daughter, about twelve years old, and she was dying. As he went, the crowds almost crushed him. ⁴³And a woman afflicted with hemorrhages for twelve years, who (had spent her whole livelihood on doctors and) was unable to be cured by anyone, ⁴⁴came up behind him and touched the tassel on his cloak. Immediately her bleeding stopped. ⁴⁵Jesus then asked, "Who touched me?" While all were denying it, Peter said, "Master, the crowds are pushing and pressing in upon you." ⁴⁶But Jesus said, "Someone has touched me; for I know that power has gone out from me. ⁴⁷When the woman realized that she had not escaped notice, she came forward trembling. Falling down before him, she explained in the presence of all the people why she had touched him and how she had been healed immediately. ⁴⁸He said to her, "Daughter, your faith has saved you; go in peace."

[49] While he was still speaking, someone from the synagogue official's house arrived and said, "Your daughter is dead; do not trouble the teacher any longer." [50] On hearing this, Jesus answered him, "Do not be afraid; just have faith and she will be saved." [51] When he arrived at the house he allowed no one to enter with him except Peter and John and James, and the child's father and mother. [52] All were weeping and mourning for her, when he said, "Do not weep any longer, for she is not dead, but sleeping." [53] And they ridiculed him, because they knew that she was dead. [54] But he took her by the hand and called to her, "Child, arise!" [55] Her breath returned and she immediately arose. He then directed that she should be given something to eat. [56] Her parents were astounded, and he instructed them to tell no one what had happened.

Luke maintains Mark's artistry in joining the two healing episodes. Jairus' request that Jesus heal his daughter is interrupted by the bold gesture of a woman who touched Jesus so that she could be healed. For the reader this interlude causes delay and builds suspense. When Jesus finally arrives at the synagogue official's house, he is told that he is too late. Undeterred, Jesus enters and restores the twelve-year-old to life.

The literary method of embedding one story (8:43–48) in another (8:40–42, 49–56) invites a comparison so that each story interprets the other. Prominent among Jewish society as a synagogue official, Jairus takes the initiative, comes to Jesus, and falls at his feet. Letting go of any claim to status, he humbly recognizes the authority of this teacher (see 8:49). Luke alone among the Synoptics notes that his dying child is his only daughter (8:42), recalling for the reader the only son of the widow from Naim (7:11–17). There is a shift in familiar relationships from mother-son in the first story to father-daughter in this one. In both instances Jesus restores life to a family stricken by grief.

While Jesus goes on his way to Jairus' home the crowds are so great that they almost crush him. Still, a nameless woman, surely weakened by the loss of menstrual blood, is able to get close enough to Jesus to touch the tassel of his cloak. Immediately—a characteristic Lukan expression in healings—her bleeding stopped. Four times in these few verses the word "touch" is used, underscoring not just the modality of healing but also the violation of purity laws. For a woman with a menstrual discharge "shall be in a state of impurity for seven days," thus preventing her from entering the Temple. Also, "anyone who touches her shall be unclean until evening" (Lv 15:19). Deciding to hide from her embarrassment no longer, this woman comes forth trembling in the presence of all the people and publicly acknowledges to Jesus that she was the one who touched him and was healed (8:47).

Neither rebuking nor shaming her, Jesus simply declares "Daughter, your faith has saved you; go in peace" (8:48), using the same healing words he spoke to the sinful woman at Simon's house (7:50). The Greek verb "to save" (sōzō), used here to mean making whole physically or releasing from physical affliction (8:50; see 17:19; 18:42; Acts 4:9; 14:9), also connotes healing as a process of salvation, a spiritual event. In Luke physical healing often symbolizes an experience of spiritual wholeness. Without hesitation this "low status" woman, rendered unclean and thus isolated from others, is restored to her place in the community.

As the story continues Jesus is told that Jairus' daughter has already died. Nonetheless, he continues on and enters his home with Peter, James, and John, along with the girl's grieving parents. Though subject to ridicule for saying that she was only sleeping, Jesus takes her hand, even though touching a corpse makes him unclean. Jesus' command, "Child, arise!" (8:54), restores her to life. The Greek term for "arise" is the same word used by Luke for the resurrection of Jesus (24:6, 34) and for the resurrection of the dead (7:22; 20:37; Acts 26:8). Although what Jairus' daughter experiences is actually a resuscitation, that is, a restoration to earthly life, the event signals the radically transformative experience of resurrection itself.

When Jesus instructs those at Jairus' home not to be afraid, but "just have faith and she will be saved" (8:50), he implicitly puts forth the faith of the "low status" hemorrhaging woman from the intervening scene as a model for the "high status" Jairus and his household. She becomes an example of faith for him, as well as those affluent members in Luke's community who may be setting themselves above their social inferiors.

In these healing stories Jesus restores two women to health. The twelve-year-old daughter is just at the age when her flow of menstrual blood, manifesting her fecundity, would begin. And the woman who has been menstruating excessively for twelve years is healed so that she can experience again the regularity of her life-giving power. Both women are restored to their family and their community. Their bodies once rendered unclean either by illness or death are now made whole.

For reflection: The moving scene of the hemorrhaging woman's encounter with Jesus is about her desperate need for healing. Like this woman, many people today have faced a chronic illness that has sapped their energy as well as financial resources. Unfortunately, stories are becoming increasingly frequent of those who have been dropped by their health insurance carrier because the cost for healthcare treatment has impacted the bottom line negatively. Acting like a ruler with the power to make a line-item veto, HMO administrators, or their minions, have too frequently erased these vulnerable ones from their rosters.

Universal access to health care is a moral challenge facing not only administrators but all members of our society. The debates about whether healthcare is a right or a privilege are moot in the face of those who suffer from untreated illnesses and unmitigated pain. What is our role in revamping our social system so that the benefits of modern medicine may be extended to all regardless of their financial resources, social position, or legal status?

The Mission of the Twelve (9:1–6)

9:1 He summoned the Twelve and gave them power and authority over all demons and to cure diseases, ²and he sent them to proclaim the kingdom of God and to heal [the sick]. ³ He said to them, "Take nothing for the journey, neither walking stick, nor sack, nor food, nor money, and let no one take a second tunic. ⁴ Whatever house you enter, stay there and leave from there. ⁵ And as for those who do not welcome you, when you leave that town, shake the dust from your feet in testimony against them." ⁶ Then they set out and went from village to village proclaiming the good news and curing diseases everywhere.

The response to Jesus' ministry at this time is enthusiastic. The crowds are coming to hear him in increasing numbers; and those in need of healing and forgiveness believe in him and are liberated. However, the religious leaders to whom the Jews would look for guidance and authority have rejected Jesus. This creates a leadership vacuum among the people. Who will serve as the leaders for renewed Israel?

Earlier in the Gospel Jesus has called the Twelve from among the disciples (6:12–16). From that moment on they have become learners, experiencing first hand how Jesus proclaimed the kingdom to the people through his teaching, healings and exorcisms. They have also witnessed the rejection of Jesus by those who could not manipulate him for their own purposes (7:31–35).

In this passage Jesus commissions the Twelve to participate fully in his purpose. They are to do what Jesus does. A little later in the story there will be a second, more developed mission to a wider number, the seventy (-two) (10:1–24). The Gospel will culminate with Jesus sending his disciples on a mission "to all the nations" (24:46–49), a world-wide mission that will be carried out in Acts.

After summoning them, Jesus confers on the Twelve "power and authority" to proclaim the kingdom of God just as he himself had been doing (4:43–44; 8:1). They were to do this in a concrete way by exercising power over all demons and by curing diseases, two hallmarks of Jesus' own ministry (4:33–41; 5:12–26; 6:6–10), which they would have directly observed or at least heard about (7:1–10, 17, 22; 8:26–39, 40–56). By his own commitment to bring the good news to others, Jesus serves as their model.

Surprisingly, Jesus places upon the Twelve very stringent conditions, much more so than was required of wandering Cynic philosophers who were recognized by their walking staff, wallet and rough cloak. The only possession allowed the Twelve was the tunic they were wearing. Taking nothing with them, they will later say to Jesus that they lacked nothing (22:35). They were to rely completely on the hospitality of those who received them, not moving from house to house, but sharing the meals and lodging of those who welcomed them. Those sent were to trust in God's providence alone.

Knowing that some would not accept them, Jesus instructed the Twelve to give a sign of rejection "in testimony against them" (9:5). Shaking the dust from one's feet is a prophetic action that indicates a radical dissociation from unbelievers (10:11; Acts 13:51). Jesus is a prophet accepted by some and rejected by others. As his disciples, the Twelve were to experience nothing different.

The Twelve carry out what they have been sent to do. Going from village to village they proclaim the good news and cure diseases everywhere (9:6). Although Luke mainly borrows this passage from Mark, he does have two editorial notes worth mentioning. The Twelve were given authority over "all" demons; and they cured diseases "everywhere" (9:6), although we will hear later that they were unable to cast the demon out of a man's only son (9:40). After their missionary journey through the villages, they come back and explain to Jesus what they had done (9:10).

For reflection: I vividly recall an experience of receiving hospitality some years ago by a rather poor family in western Ireland. Living in a simple three-room dwelling, two with dirt floors, the other rough concrete, they seemed to be very happy and at peace. On their walls were a few religious symbols and two pictures, one of Pope John XXIII and the other of John F. Kennedy. They warmly welcomed me and my fellow travelers burdened with our heavy suitcases. For three days they had been awaiting our arrival. The table had been set with special foods the children would only see at Christmas. The strength of their faith and the simplicity of their lifestyle served as a powerful witness to us about what matters.

This passage is not so much about asceticism, as it is about proclaiming the good news unencumbered by baggage that may get in the way. It is about trusting in God's providence, knowing that some will be open to God's reign and others will not.

For church leaders and all believers it is a poignant reminder about the need to proclaim the sovereignty of God with authority, since God's emissaries have received power over demons and the gift of healing. The demons of today may look very different than during Jesus' time. The demons may be any powers or principalities that place profits over human needs, and societal structures that favor the few over the many. This is where the kingdom of justice and peace is to be proclaimed. Some may be led to conversion of heart, and others may not. Nonetheless, God's kingdom is to be proclaimed without faltering.

Peter's Confession, Passion Prediction, and Discipleship (9:18–27)

The word is spreading. Herod hears about all that is happening. Perplexed, he kept trying to see Jesus (9:7–9). The crowds keep coming. Jesus continues to receive them and speaks to them about the kingdom of God, healing those who need to be cured (9:11). At the end of the day, the Twelve, who had just been instructed to accept hospitality from others, are reluctant to extend it to the crowd. But Jesus persists and feeds the multitude so that "they all ate and were satisfied" (9:17). After this Jesus withdraws with the disciples to a solitary place.

[18] Once when Jesus was praying in solitude, and the disciples were with him, he asked them, "Who do the crowds say that I am?" [19] They said in reply, "John the Baptist; others, Elijah; still others, 'One of the ancient prophets has arisen.' " [20] Then he said to them, "But who do you say that I am?" Peter said in reply, "The Messiah of God." [21] He rebuked them and directed them not to tell this to anyone. [22] He said, "The Son of Man must suffer greatly and be rejected by the elders, the chief priests, and the scribes, and be killed and on the third day be raised." [23] Then he said to all, "If anyone wishes to come after me, he must deny himself and take up his cross daily and follow me. [24] For whoever wishes to save his life will lose it, but whoever loses his life for my sake will save it. [25] What profit is there for one to gain the whole world yet lose or forfeit himself? [26] Whoever is ashamed of me and of my words, the Son of Man will be ashamed of when he comes in his glory and in the glory of the Father and of the holy angels. [27] Truly I say to you, there are some standing here who will not taste death until they see the kingdom of God."

In this story the true identity of Jesus and the nature of discipleship are closely related, and lead into the next episode, the manifestation of Jesus in his glory. Knowing who Jesus is, especially coming to grips with the necessity of his rejection, suffering and death, directly informs the way of life to be embraced by all his disciples. For those who would follow in the steps of the master the demands are great.

The scene unfolds with Jesus at prayer with his disciples apart from the crowds. In the Gospel of Luke the mention of Jesus praying signals that an important event is about to happen. While we are not told the content of Jesus' prayer, the unfolding dialogue suggests that Jesus may have been pondering his own calling. Having already experienced some success among the crowds, yet having felt the painful rejection by the religious leaders of his day—who ought to know about the things of God—Jesus may have been seeking divine enlightenment.

It is not inconceivable that Jesus was searching for some insight to such questions as: "Who am I in the sight of God?" "What path am I being asked to follow?" "What impact will the unfolding of my life have on those who have come with me?" and "How am I to instruct them about the demands they will face as disciples?" Seeking guidance for whatever uncertainties he may have encountered, Jesus sought God's wisdom.

Jesus asks the disciples about his identity: "Who do the crowds say I am?" The purpose of Jesus' query may well have been to assist the disciples in deepening their own understanding of who he really is. The responses given to Jesus were the same as those offered to Herod (9:7–9). By referring to Jesus as "one of the ancient prophets" who "has arisen," Luke artfully hints at Jesus' own glory to be revealed (see 9:26; 24:26).

Replying as the spokesperson for the disciples, Peter confidently answers that Jesus is "The Messiah of God" (9:20). The Greek term *Christos*, translated as "Messiah," literally means "anointed one." Jesus has already been announced as the Messiah (2:11); then Jesus proclaims this about himself (4:18); and now Peter, having observed Jesus' power to heal the afflicted, comes through with the correct answer. Unlike the Markan Jesus who rebuffs Peter (Mk 8:33) and the Matthean Jesus who praises Peter (Mt 16:17–19), the Lukan Jesus rebukes them all and orders them to keep silent (9:21).

Why? Neither Peter nor the disciples really understand what it means for Jesus to be the Messiah. Jesus explains that the Son of Man must suffer, be killed, and then on the third day be raised. This is the first of three passion predictions in Luke's Gospel (9:22; 9:43–45; and 18:31–34). If Jesus is to be the Messiah, this term must be understood as one who will suffer, something the disciples do not yet understand. Therefore, Jesus commands them not to say anything to others until they get the real picture.

Many, from brilliant theologians to simple people of faith, have tried to come to terms with a suffering Messiah. Like the other evangelists, Luke affirms that this must happen. The Greek verb in 9:22, *dei* ("must," "it is necessary"), means that God's plan for redemption must unfold through the cross. Jesus confesses that he must "suffer greatly" (9:22). He will also be rejected by three authoritative groups: the elders, the chief priests, and the scribes, who together make up the Sanhedrin, the ruling court of the Jewish nation. Already the disciples have had glimpses of growing resistance to Jesus (5:21, 30, 32; 6:2, 11; 7:29–30, 39, 49). Shockingly new to them is that their Messiah will be killed and then raised up. How will they deal with this surprising disclosure?

In a series of sharply worded sayings Jesus explains what discipleship means. He addresses "all" of them—disciples and readers of the Gospel (9:23)—who wish to continue to come after him. The aorist tense of the Greek verb for "come" means continued action. Discipleship is not a one-time decision, but an ongoing matter. The essential pattern for any Christians is to deny oneself and to take up one's cross daily. Adding the word "daily" to what is in Mark, the Lukan Jesus says that being a disciple is not just being ready to accept a martyr's death, but involves a day-by-day acceptance of the cross, considered by non-believers to be "foolishness" (1 Cor 1:18, 23).

In contrast to conventional wisdom Jesus asserts that the person who "loses" one's life (literally "soul"), will save it (9:24). Using economic terms Jesus explains that even if a person becomes tremendously wealthy and gains the "whole world," that will not "profit" for the person loses his/her soul in the process (9:25). Jesus attacks the very root of the unholy alliance between personal wealth and security.

The refusal to be loyal to Jesus and to the kingdom values he preaches is to shame him, rather than honor him. There is a direct consequence to this: the Son of Man will be ashamed of that person when he comes into his glory. Both judgment and hope are expressed: judgment for those who fail to embrace the cross, and hope, because the Son of Man, who must suffer and die, is also destined for glory. Ultimate glory will be revealed in the resurrection. Since the disciples are to be like their Master, the Messiah, they too will experience glory on the other side of the cross they daily embrace.

For reflection: This passage gets right at the heart of who Jesus is and what it means to be a disciple. With the many challenges to the Christian way in today's world, one does not have to go out looking for crosses to carry. Each believer who experiences in community and in personal prayer the living presence of God is aware of the great demands placed upon one's self to live faithfully as a Christian. The market society in which we operate continually shouts to all who would hear: look out for number one. Security is to be found in accumulating wealth. Put your energy into looking out for yourself ("save oneself") for no one else will.

To be a Christian is to live with counter-cultural values. The famous prayer, attributed to Francis of Assisi, captured this well, "Lord, make me an instrument of your peace." To be a disciple is to act with the conviction that "It is in giving that we receive."

Transfiguration of Jesus (9:28–36)

²⁸ About eight days after he said this, he took Peter, John, and James and went up the mountain to pray. ²⁹ While he was praying his face changed in appearance and his clothing became dazzling white. ³⁰ And behold, two men were conversing with him, Moses and Elijah, ³¹ who appeared in glory and spoke of his exodus that he was going to accomplish in Jerusalem. ³² Peter and his companions had been overcome by sleep, but becoming fully awake, they saw his glory and the two men standing with him. ³³ As they were about to part

from him, Peter said to Jesus, "Master, it is good that we are here; let us make three tents, one for you, one for Moses, and one for Elijah." But he did not know what he was saying. [34]While he was still speaking, a cloud came and cast a shadow over them, and they became frightened when they entered the cloud. [35]Then from the cloud came a voice that said, "This is my chosen Son; listen to him." [36] After the voice had spoken, Jesus was found alone. They fell silent and did not at that time tell anyone what they had seen.

In the transfiguration story Luke uses the rich imagery of face, garment, light, cloud, glory, voice and mountain to impress upon the disciples the divine status of Jesus. For those who may have misgivings about Jesus' previous words on suffering and the cross, Luke closely connects this passage to the sayings on discipleship ("after he said this," 9:28). The transfiguration confirms that the teacher is indeed the Son of God, and that there is triumph beyond suffering. This mountain top experience offers a momentary glimpse of future glory, while emphasizing that the path to glory involves the suffering of God's chosen son.

This extraordinary event takes place during one of Jesus' customary prayer experiences. He prays while three of his chosen disciples, Peter, James, and John, slumber. During his prayer Jesus personally experiences a brief glimmer of glory. His face changes and his clothing becomes "dazzling white." White is a symbol of joy and celebration. The imagery recalls the Ancient One from Daniel whose "clothing was snow bright" (Dn 7:9). Looking ahead, this imagery anticipates Jesus' resurrection when two men (angels?) appear in "dazzling garments" (24:4) as well as the ascension of Jesus also witnessed by two men "dressed in white garments" (Acts 1:10).

On the mountain Jesus converses with Moses and Elijah, each of whom helps us to understand who this Galilean peasant is. Moses is the one who announced that there will be a prophet like him whom God will raise up (Dt 18:15), a theme taken up by Luke in Acts (3:22). Like Jesus Moses ascended a mountain where he was enveloped by a cloud and heard God's voice (Ex 24:15–16; 34:5). Elijah was already presented as a model for Jesus' ministry (Lk 4:25–26; 7:11–17). Like Jesus who was "taken up" (9:51, see 2 Kgs 2:11), Elijah is to appear before the time of fulfillment (Mal 3:23). Together Moses and Elijah represent the law and the prophets who witness to God's purposes that are fulfilled in Jesus (24:27, 44).

Only Luke among the evangelists tells us about their conversation with Jesus. Moses and Elijah were talking about Jesus' exodus. Certainly recalling the liberating plight of the Hebrews from Egypt to the promised land, the exodus in Luke 9:31 refers collectively to Jesus' imminent journey to Jerusalem (9:51), to his departure from this life, and finally to his resurrection and ascension, when he will enter into his glory (24:26). Jesus' exodus is his journey to liberation that will establish the kingdom of God for all people.

When Peter begins to wake up he sees the glory, though he missed the heavenly conversation. He suggests to his Master that they set up three tents to capture the moment. Mistakenly thinking that Jesus has already entered into his glory, unaware that Jesus has yet to suffer, Peter hardly realizes what he is saying.

At this moment a cloud descends upon Peter and his silent companions. They become afraid. Blocking their vision, the cloud symbolizes God's presence. For out of this cloud they hear the heavenly voice declare: "This is my chosen Son; listen to him." At his baptism the voice spoke to Jesus about his divine sonship (3:22), and now this is announced to the disciples. Since Jesus is God's son, they are to listen to him, to hear what he has just said about his own suffering and death; they are to take to heart his teaching about the cross and discipleship (9:22–26). The command to "listen to him," also means to pay close attention to all that Jesus will teach them on the journey to Jerusalem (9:51–19:27).

For reflection: Sometimes in the spiritual journey, perhaps during a time of prayer, those who seek to follow Jesus will have a mountain top experience. Similar to the disciples, this may be a momentary glimpse of the resurrected Jesus. Experiences like this can bring great comfort, especially during times of trial. Unlike the somnolent disciples, we are encouraged to wake up to these experiences when they occur, and to listen to whatever God has to tell us.

If we have never had a mountain top experience of the living Jesus, it is probably not helpful to think that this will never happen, or to feel unworthy. It may well be that our challenge is to remain alert to the ways in which God manifests the face of Jesus to us in our day-to-day life. Mother Teresa is a good example. She often spoke about how she saw the face of Jesus in the poorest of the poor. If we believe that we are the body of Christ, then Jesus is indeed present in each member of his body with whom we come into contact. How do you see and hear God manifested in those around you?

Can you recall a time in the past week, or the past year, when you were aware of God's presence? What was this like? Who was there? How did you feel? What impact has this experience had on you since? These experiences are not so much to be captured by enclosing them in a tent. Rather, they are to be seen as mystery to be entered into.

IV
Jesus' Journey to Jerusalem
(9:51–13:21)

Several times in the Acts of the Apostles Luke refers to the Christian movement as "the Way" (Acts 9:2; 19:9, 23; 22:4; 24:22). It is the way of life for all those who respond to the call to follow Jesus. The Way has both a literal and a metaphorical sense. Metaphorically, it is a life of discipleship. To follow the Way is to pattern one's life after that of Jesus. It means to incorporate into our way of being the values of God's kingdom.

The Way also has a literal meaning. Luke's two-volume work consists of many journeys, some quite extensive. Acts narrates four journeys of Paul, the last one to Rome, a journey that represents the spread of the Christian movement "to the ends of the earth" (1:8). Another extended journey occurs at the heart of Luke's Gospel. Unfolding in ten chapters from Luke 9:51 to 19:27, this section is often called Jesus' travel narrative. It begins in Galilee where Jesus has been teaching and healing in the early part of the Gospel (chapters 3–9) and ends with his arrival in Jerusalem.

Along the way Jesus teaches his disciples, the crowds, and the people about God's kingdom. Among those who hear this teaching are Jesus' opponents, the scribes and the Pharisees. To those who respond positively, Jesus gives instructions about discipleship. Some from among the crowds convert, some hesitate, and others outright reject Jesus' prophetic invitation. While there are various healing stories along the journey to Jerusalem (11:14; 13:10–17; 14:1–6; 17:11–19; 18:35–43), most of the time Jesus is teaching.

97

The travel narrative begins with Luke's formal announcement of Jesus' departure for Jerusalem, the encounter with Samaritans, and the conditional response of would-be followers (9:51–62). Three times in this section we are reminded that Jesus is on his way (9:52, 56, 57; see also 10:38; 13:33).

Departure for Jerusalem, Samaritan Rejection and Would-be Followers (9:51–62)

[51] When the days for his being taken up were fulfilled, he resolutely determined to journey to Jerusalem, [52] and he sent messengers ahead of him. On the way they entered a Samaritan village to prepare for his reception there, [53] but they would not welcome him because the destination of his journey was Jerusalem. [54] When the disciples James and John saw this they asked, "Lord, do you want us to call down fire from heaven to consume them?" [55] Jesus turned and rebuked them, [56] and they journeyed to another village.

[57] As they were proceeding on their journey someone said to him, "I will follow you wherever you go." [58] Jesus answered him, "Foxes have dens and birds of the sky have nests, but the Son of Man has nowhere to rest his head." [59] And to another he said, "Follow me." But he replied, "[Lord,] let me go first and bury my father." [60] But he answered him, "Let the dead bury their dead. But you, go and proclaim the kingdom of God." [61] And another said, "I will follow you, Lord, but first let me say farewell to my family at home." [62] [To him] Jesus said, "No one who sets a hand to the plow and looks to what was left behind is fit for the kingdom of God."

The main themes marking the start of the journey are the "taking up" of Jesus, the fulfillment of God's will and Jesus' obedient response. Like Elijah before him, taken to heaven in a whirlwind (2 Kings 2:1), Jesus was also to be "taken up" (9:51; see Acts 1:2). With a meaning very similar to that of "exodus" (9:31), the *analempsis* ("taking up") of Jesus refers collectively to his suffering, death, resurrection, and ascension. This also includes the Pentecost event, for the sending of the Holy Spirit occurs at the time of fulfillment (Acts 2:1; 2:33–35). Accomplishing all this and bringing all to completion is God, the faithful one (see Lk 1:1; 2:22).

At this divinely appointed time, Jesus "resolutely determined" to head up to Jerusalem. The Greek verb literally means "set his face" or even "hardened his face." This expression is used when God or one of the prophets speaks words of judgment (Jer 21:10; Ez 6:2; 13:17; 21:2, 7–8). In this context it means that Jesus goes toward Jerusalem as a prophet despite all opposition.

Jesus sends messengers ahead of him (literally, "before his face") to arrange for hospitality and probably to begin preaching. Echoing the role of the Baptist about whom the Lord said, "Behold, I am sending my messenger ahead of you" (literally, "before your face," 7:27), the disciples are to prepare for Jesus' coming into a Samaritan village. They are, however, not welcomed.

Geographically, Samaria lies between Galilee and Judea, and anyone going to Jerusalem would have to pass through that territory. Jews and Samaritans were bitterly opposed to each other (see Jn 4:9). Having their own sanctuary on Mt. Gerizim, the Samaritans refused to recognize the Jerusalem Temple on Mt. Zion, and thus would be inhospitable to anyone going there. There was little tolerance on either side for cultural or religious diversity.

Seeking a green light from Jesus, James and John wanted to "call down fire from heaven" as an act of vengeance. This is the same destructive force that Elijah used twice against troops from Samaria (2 Kgs 1:10, 12). Refusing to allow what Elijah had done, Jesus practiced his own teaching of non-retaliation against enemies (6:27–29). Instead of permitting such an abuse of power, he went on with his disciples to another village. Later along the journey, Jesus uses the Samaritans as positive examples of the call to discipleship (10:29–37; 17:11–19). And in

Acts, first Philip, then James and John preached the good news to many in Samaria bringing great joy (Acts 8:4–25).

The opposition to Jesus' teaching mission at the onset of his travel narrative recalls the rejection that he faced at the beginning of his public ministry in Nazareth (4:16–30). Both times God's plan for Jesus to bring the good news of the kingdom meets with rejection and hostility. Whether or not Jesus was disheartened, we do not know. What is clear is that he faithfully continued in obedience to the divine plan.

Journeying forward Jesus meets three potential followers. The first and third of these volunteer to follow him—an unusual occurrence in the Gospel—the second Jesus invites. To each of the three Jesus utters a proverb about the unconditional nature of discipleship. With enthusiasm the first eagerly professes to follow "wherever you go" (9:57). Rather than offer encouragement, Jesus replies with a warning. Unlike foxes and birds who have resting places, "the Son of Man has nowhere to rest his head" (9:58). Although offered hospitality on occasion (10:38–42), Jesus is mainly homeless. The security that animals and birds are able to arrange for themselves is not guaranteed to the disciple.

The person invited by Jesus seems willing, but he voices what sounds like a reasonable request, the desire to bury his father first. This need to fulfill such a pressing family obligation would appear to be required by the commandment: "Honor your father and your mother" (Ex 20:12; see also Tb 4:3–4; 6:14–15; 14:12–13). It is a prime duty. Thus, Jesus' response to let the dead bury their dead seems perplexing. Does this mean to let the spiritually dead bury the physically dead? The command to "go and proclaim the kingdom of God" (9:60) is what the apostles were instructed to do (9:2) and anticipates what the seventy (-two) will be sent out for (10:9,11).

Who could fault the request of the third person to say farewell to the family at home before following Jesus (9:61)? Out in the field plowing, Elisha wanted to do something similar—go home to kiss his father—before he followed after Elijah (1 Kgs

19:19–21). Jesus, however, denies the would-be disciple's request and responds with a harsh proverb from agricultural life: "No one who sets a hand to the plow and looks to what was left behind is fit for the kingdom of God" (9:62). The issue is not a fear of plowing crooked rows, but an uncompromising commitment to the kingdom.

The latter two cases involve familial obligations. Jesus' teaching is that loyalty to family is not to distract in any way from the call to discipleship. Jesus renders even harsher sayings later on about family division: "From now on a household of five will be divided, three against two and two against three" (12:52); about hatred: "If any one comes to me without hating his father and mother . . . he cannot be my disciple" (14:26); and about betrayal: "You will even be handed over by parents, brothers, relatives, and friends, and they will put some of you to death" (21:16). Even apart from Jesus' use of hyperbole and exaggeration to make a point, these sayings impress upon us that family members who are attracted to the Way could be ostracized by their own because of their faith.

For reflection: This passage is powerful, demanding, and disturbing. Jesus' own unwavering determination to follow God's plan is an example for all believers. Surely, Jesus is one who put his hand to the plow and never looked back. Most disciples, including us, probably cannot say that. Nonetheless, that does not mean that we should be like James and John and call down "fire from heaven" on those who stumble along the way or, to change the metaphor, happen to plow crooked rows. Even less, should we castigate ourselves, believing that we are to be punished with fire from heaven, whatever form that might take.

Yes, the call to discipleship is demanding, and requires sacrifice. Sometimes this will cause division in the family. A few years ago while giving a course at a theological seminary in Hong Kong, I taught several who were relatively new converts to Christianity. Often they came from families where a combination of Buddhist, Confucian, Taoist, and folk religions were practiced. Upon their becoming Christian, it was not unusual for their families to shun them or even to ostracize them. Although this created a fair amount of angst among the new converts, their faith remained strong supported by the new ties they developed among the family of believers.

There may be some today who enter the Rite of Christian Initiation of Adults program without the support of family and friends. Hopefully, these inquirers into the faith will find in the community of believers a wider family of brothers and sisters bound together by their desire to "hear the word of God and act on it" (8:21). What opposition have you faced because of your faith, and where have you sought support?

Mission of the Seventy-two and their Return (10:1–20)

[10:1] After this the Lord appointed seventy[-two] others whom he sent ahead of him in pairs to every town and place he intended to visit. [2] He said to them, "The harvest is abundant but the laborers are few; so ask the master of the harvest to send out laborers for his harvest. [3] Go on your way; behold, I am sending you like lambs among wolves. [4] Carry no money bag, no sack, no sandals; and greet no one along the way. [5] Into whatever house you enter, first say, 'Peace to this household.' [6] If a peaceful person lives there, your peace will rest on him; but if not, it will return to you. [7] Stay in the same house and eat and drink what is offered to you, for the laborer deserves his payment. Do not move about from one house to another. [8] Whatever town you enter and they welcome you, eat what is set before you, [9] cure the sick in it and say to them, 'The kingdom of God is at hand for you.' [10] Whatever town you enter and they do not receive you, go out into the streets and say, [11] 'The dust of your town that clings to our feet, even that we shake off against you.' Yet know this: the kingdom of God is at hand. [12] I tell you, it will be more tolerable for Sodom on that day than for that town.

[13] "Woe to you, Chorazin! Woe to you, Bethsaida! For if the mighty deeds done in your midst had been done in Tyre and Sidon, they would long ago have repented, sitting in sackcloth and ashes. [14] But it will be more tolerable for Tyre and Sidon at the judgment than for you. [15] And as for you, Capernaum, 'Will you be exalted to heaven? You will go down to the netherworld.' [16] Whoever listens to you listens to me. Whoever rejects you rejects me. And whoever rejects me rejects the one who sent me."

[17] The seventy[-two] returned rejoicing, and said, "Lord, even the demons are subject to us because of your name." [18] Jesus said, "I have observed Satan fall like lightning from the sky. [19] Behold, I have given you the power 'to tread upon serpents' and scorpions and upon the full force of the enemy and nothing will harm you. [20] Nevertheless, do not rejoice because the spirits are subject to you, but rejoice because your names are written in heaven."

This is the second of two missionary mandates in Luke. The Twelve have already been sent (9:1–6), but their number is evidently not sufficient to carry out the urgent task of preaching the kingdom (10:9, 11). This larger group of seventy-two, whose instructions are given in a more extended account, is entrusted with a mission equally as important: to cure the sick and to proclaim the reign of God (10:9). This passage unfolds in three parts: the commissioning and instructions (10:1–12), the judgment upon unrepentant towns (10:13–16), and the joyful return of the missionaries (10:17–10).

First, a word about the number commissioned. Some ancient Greek manuscripts read "seventy," others "seventy-two." There is no clear indication as to which is the original reading, so the NAB represents this ambiguity as "seventy[-two]." Two Old Testament texts influence the number. In Genesis 10:2–31 there are seventy (Hebrew Text) or seventy-two (Septuagint [LXX]—Greek text) listed in the table of nations. In Numbers 11:16–17 the Lord instructs Moses to select seventy from the elders of Israel to receive the spirit, and later two others are also included (Nm 11:26). The number seventy-two would indicate in Luke 10 a mission to the world of nations by spirit-filled disciples.

They are sent two by two to every place Jesus intended to visit. Two is the biblically required number to bear witness to the truth (Dt 19:15). Going in pairs they would also be able to provide mutual support especially during times of rejection. In Acts Paul and Barnabas are the most well-known team, but there are also the church leaders Aquila and Priscilla, a married couple. A model of evangelizing in pairs remains a wise and viable option in the contemporary church.

Even though the Lord appoints seventy-two, his first instruction to them is to ask the harvest master to send out even more laborers. Part of their task may have been to identify other potential proclaimers of the kingdom. Instructed to travel light, the disciples will face dangers and rejection as happened in Samaria (9:53), for they are being sent like lambs among the wolves. As disciples of Jesus they are to herald a new era of peace when the wolf will be the guest of the lamb (Is 11:6; 65:25).

There is a progression from a home-based mission (10:5–7) to that of the cities (10:8–11). The disciples are to bring a message of peace to the homes. This is a powerful greeting (see 24:36), and will be received by the peaceful person (literally, "son of peace," 10:6). Peace is a hallmark of salvation offered to Israel (1:79; 2:14, 29; Acts 10:36) and beyond to all peoples. Jesus' triumphal end of this journey in Jerusalem will be momentarily celebrated as a time of "peace in heaven" (19:38), although there is certainly no calm in that city during the days leading up to his death.

The seventy-two are not to go around as beggars for the laborer deserves payment (10:7). They are to receive hospitality in homes—eating, drinking, sharing life and thus building community. Some towns will welcome them, others will not. Those who will not are to be given a stern verbal warning and to receive a sign of judgment: the shaking off of dust from the disciples' feet. Yet, even these villages are to hear that God's kingdom is near. Those towns who reject the messengers are judged to be worse than Sodom, a corrupt city punished by God (Gen 19:1–29). Three cities in particular are singled out for severe judgment: Chorazin, Bethsaida, and Capernaum (10:13–16). Even though the crowds were impressed with the mighty deeds Jesus worked in Capernaum (4:42), what is required of them is repentance.

After the warnings about rejection, the reader might expect the messengers to return despondent. Instead, they come back jubilant, reporting to their Lord that surprisingly even the demons were subject to them (10:17; see 9:1–2). They were able to do this because of his name, a name that represents power and authority (9:49; Acts 3:16; 16:18). Jesus interprets this as Satan falling like lightning from the sky (see Rv 12:7–9). Such dramatic imagery means that as the kingdom of God is established, the prince of demons along with all its forms, symbolized by serpents and scorpions, is being defeated. Impressed as the seventy-two might be with their power over demons, they are naturally told by Jesus to rejoice not in this but because their names are written in heaven (10:20). To be inscribed in the heavenly books (Ex 32:32–33; Ps 69:29; 139:16; Phil 4:3; Heb 12:23; Rev 3:5) is a sign that they are on the side of God whose kingdom rules over all.

For reflection: There are several themes in this passage that are instructive for the church today. One is the wisdom of evangelists and witnesses of God's kingdom working together, at least in pairs and not as lone rangers. Through mutual collaboration a rich combination of spiritual gifts can be put at the service of the gospel. Those whose hearts may not be reached by one person, may well be touched by a different approach. A second theme is that of building up small, home-based communities. Faith sharing in the intimate environment of a home can be very enriching spiritually, complementing the larger parish experience. Reflecting on the scriptures together, sharing your experiences on how the Gospel has influenced your life, seeking discernment for important decisions to be made and celebrating the Lord's eucharistic presence are all rich sources of God's grace. This means, of course, that church leaders ought to be encouraged and not threatened by flourishing faith-based home communities. If you do not belong to a faith-sharing community, might you be called to begin one?

The Parable of the Good Samaritan (10:25–37)

[25] There was a scholar of the law who stood up to test him and said, "Teacher, what must I do to inherit eternal life?" [26] Jesus said to him, "What is written in the law? How do you read it?" [27] He said in reply, "You shall love the Lord, your God, with all your heart, with all your being, with all your strength, and with all your mind, and your neighbor as yourself." [28] He replied to him, "You have answered correctly; do this and you will live."

[29] But because he wished to justify himself, he said to Jesus, "And who is my neighbor?" [30] Jesus replied, "A man fell victim to robbers as he went down from Jerusalem to Jericho. They stripped and beat him and went off leaving him half-dead. [31] A priest happened to be going down that road, but when he saw him, he passed by on the opposite side. [32] Likewise a Levite came to the place, and when he saw him, he passed by on the opposite side. [33] But a Samaritan traveler who came upon him was moved with compassion at the sight. [34] He approached the victim, poured oil and wine over his wounds and bandaged them. Then he lifted him up on his own animal, took him to an inn and cared for him. [35] The next day he took out two silver coins and gave them to the innkeeper with the instruction, 'Take care of him. If you spend more than what I have given you, I shall repay you on my way back.' [36] Which of these three, in your opinion, was neighbor to the robbers' victim?" [37] He answered, "The one who treated him with mercy." Jesus said to him, "Go and do likewise."

The Good Samaritan is one of the most compelling parables in Luke's Gospel. Jesus tells this transformative story as the centerpiece of his reply to a scribe's question: "Who is my neighbor?" The dialogue is initiated by this scholar of the Jewish law who comes to test Jesus. With suspicious and hostile intent similar to other scholars of the law (7:29–30), he approaches Jesus with the question: "What must I do to inherit eternal life?" (10:25; see 18:18).

In the Jewish scriptures the land is often named as an inheritance from God to the people. The inheritance motif is applied in the New Testament to either the kingdom of God or to eternal life (1 Cor 6:9–10; 15:50; Gal 5:19–21). To the scribe's challenge, Jesus replies as an engaging teacher with a counter-question about what is written in the law.

Demonstrating an accurate knowledge of the law, the lawyer answers by citing Leviticus 19:18 and Deuteronomy 6:5, a verse used by Jews in their daily prayers. In giving the lawyer's reply, Luke combines these two great commandments from the Old Testament into a single, forceful mandate: "You shall love . . . " (see Mt 22:37–39; Mk 12:30–31). The fourfold "all your heart, being, strength, and mind" underscores the radical and unconditional love required of the whole person for the Creator.

Regarding the latter part of the great commandment, it is often emphasized from a psychological perspective that one cannot love the neighbor unless one has a love for self. While this is undoubtedly true, the love of neighbor mandate in the biblical context assumes that people do love themselves. This, then, is to be the standard for love of others. Having answered correctly, the lawyer is commended by Jesus, for loving God and neighbor will bring eternal life. Emphasizing the importance of putting the love command into practice, Jesus asserts: "Do this and you will live" (10:28).

Aiming to justify himself, the lawyer continues to test Jesus by asking: "And who is my neighbor?" The Greek word for neighbor, *plesion*, literally means "one who is near." This scribe may have known that according to his own scriptures neighbor is restricted to one's fellow countryman (Lv 19:18), although he may also have been aware that its meaning may be extended to include the stranger or resident alien (Lv 19:33–34). Challenging the lawyer to grapple with his own question, Jesus tells a provocative parable that will, with a surprise twist, be turned on its head.

On the road from Jerusalem to Jericho, a drop in elevation of some three thousand two hundred feet, a man falls victim to violence leaving him stripped, beaten, and apparently dead. Given the geographical location, he was probably a Judean. In quick succession three possible helpers appear on the scene. The first two, a priest and a Levite, represent members of a class who were expected to be models of loving one's neighbor. However, restricted by purity laws from being defiled by what seemed to be a corpse (Lv 21:1–3), they go to the opposite side of the road, not allowing themselves to come close enough to even assess the case.

The attentive reader might expect the third passerby to be a lay Israelite. Astonishingly, however, it is a Samaritan traveler, who, as one despised by the Jews, is himself at risk on this dangerous, mainly deserted, Judean route. Closely approaching the near lifeless victim, he is moved with compassion (10:33). The vivid Greek verb, *splagchnizomai*, means to be moved physically from one's innermost bowels, and is used of Jesus, who is "moved with pity" when he sees the widow of Naim whose only son just died (7:13).

Going beyond a simple emotional reaction, the Samaritan acts, putting both himself and his possessions at the disposal of this unfortunate victim. Applying oil, wine, and bandages, he physically picks up this man, puts him on his animal, and takes him to an inn where he cared for him. Instructing the innkeeper to do the same, he offers to pay for any additional expenses. Many, especially those in healthcare, have looked at the Samaritan as one of the first paramedics who courageously came to the rescue of a man whose life hung in the balance.

Now Jesus is ready to ask his question, not the expected, "Which of these responded to this victim as neighbor?" but "Who was neighbor to him?" Not bringing himself to say "Samaritan," the lawyer replied: "The one who treated him with mercy." The Samaritan, the enemy of the Jews, is neighbor, and thus, a member of God's people. The lawyer is astonished to realize that his neighbor is his hated enemy, the hero of the story—the Samaritan. Responding with a compassionate heart, this Samaritan was the only traveler who stopped to help the injured party abandoned by two Jewish leaders. The scholar of the law is called to love this enemy, the one who may be there to help him when he, too, is in need of rescue.

For reflection: On the surface this is a compelling story about the superiority of compassionate love over confining legalism, a story about bountiful mercy toward the one in need. The starting point for the committed believer is not to ask who belongs to God's people, and thus qualifies as the neighbor to be loved, but rather to see that all people, even one's enemy are neighbors. The disciple of Jesus must be willing to be taught by the enemy what love of neighbor means. This is humbling, this is grace.

Once our understanding of neighbor is expansive enough to include even the despised, then the challenge is to translate compassionate feelings into action. This means to put our person and our resources at the service of the one in need. However, even with this attitude, there is the danger of approaching the other with a condescending paternalism. The danger is to treat the other as object, the beneficiary of our generosity. The intent to "help" someone can become more self-serving than a moment of grace for either oneself or the other.

The parable of the Good Samaritan arouses us from our moral slumber and invites us to identify honestly who our enemy might be: One from a different ethnicity? The person from a another race? A different faith group? "An undocumented" resident? A person living with AIDS? Or to bring into one focus the marginalized: an African American single parent on welfare dying with AIDS? This parable invites us to allow such a person to be neighbor to us, thus freeing us from self-justifying thoughts and actions. In an encounter of this kind where one dares to meet in what Martin Buber calls an I-Thou relationship, there is redemption—there is grace.

Martha and Mary (10:38–42)

[38] As they continued their journey he entered a village where a woman whose name was Martha welcomed him. [39] She had a sister named Mary [who] sat beside the Lord at his feet listening to him speak. [40] Martha, burdened with much serving, came to him and said, "Lord, do you not care that my sister has left me by myself to do the serving? Tell her to help me." [41] The Lord said to her in reply, "Martha, Martha, you are anxious and worried about many things. [42] There is need of only one thing. Mary has chosen the better part and it will not be taken from her."

Continuing on his journey, Jesus enters the home of two sisters, Martha and Mary, and receives their gracious hospitality. Martha's initial response in welcoming Jesus is commendable. By her hospitality she serves as a model for others. In terms of the missionary instructions, Martha and Mary can be called "daughters of peace" (see 10:6), even though some friction develops between them about the roles they assume. Notice that in entering this home Jesus transgresses cultural norms, for he is apparently alone teaching these two women in privacy.

Sitting at Jesus' feet, Mary is in a position that acknowledges his authority (7:38; 8:35, 41; 17:16; Acts 4:35, 37; 5:2; 22:3). It is remarkable for a woman to assume this posture of discipleship. Mary neglects domestic duties so that she can learn to be a disciple by hearing her Master. She attentively listens to Jesus, literally, "to his word" (10:39). This does not mean passivity on her part. For Mary to put aside her culturally expected role of preparing food required bold action that did not win the approval of her sister who was burdened with much serving. Martha's question, "Lord, do you not care . . . ?" comes across as an accusation. Perhaps feeling self-absorbed and resentful, she was not pleased that Mary left her to do the work. Doubtlessly needing help, Martha tried to have Jesus intervene and coerce Mary back into her expected role. Jesus, however, does not conform to her expectations.

Calling her twice by name, as if trying to get Martha's attention on her way back into the kitchen, Jesus names her anxiety and worry. The verb, "to be troubled," can mean to put oneself in an uproar. Clearly aware that Martha is not in a good space, Jesus does not rescue her. He does, however, remind her that only one thing is needed, namely, to pay attention to the guest rather than to be dutiful about domestic performance. What counts is to be like the rich soil that receives the word of God and to "embrace it with a generous and good heart" (8:15). All the rest is optional. For that reason Mary has chosen the better part.

For reflection: This moving scene, tender yet not without tension, reminds Luke's community about the importance of offering hospitality to the guest, especially to the traveling missionaries. On another level this encounter teaches that the task of hospitality ought not distract the host from being present to the one who brings the message. Hospitality means to receive the other, being open to how the surprise visitor may reveal God's presence in a word, a gesture, or even in respectful silence.

Many have seen in this episode an image of a nascent house church. It is probable that in Luke's time there were other women like Martha and Mary, such as Lydia in Acts (16:14–15, 40), who were leaders of small faith communities.

What opportunities have women taken in your faith community to listen closely to God's word and to act on it, especially in leadership positions? What are the unmet needs? What are the obstacles? Are there culturally-defined role expectations that impede the active listening to God's word—the one thing that is important—and acting on it?

The Lord's Prayer and Teachings on Prayer (11:1–13)

11:1 He was praying in a certain place, and when he had finished, one of his disciples said to him, "Lord, teach us to pray just as John taught his disciples." ² He said to them, "When you pray, say:

Father, hallowed be your name,

your kingdom come.

³ Give us each day our daily bread

⁴ and forgive us our sins

for we ourselves forgive everyone in debt to us,

and do not subject us to the final test."

⁵ And he said to them, "Suppose one of you has a friend to whom he goes at midnight and says, 'Friend, lend me three loaves of bread, ⁶ for a friend of mine has arrived at my house from a journey and I have nothing to offer him,' ⁷ and he says in reply from within, 'Do not bother me; the door has already been locked and my children and I are already in bed. I cannot get up to give you anything.' ⁸ I tell you, if he does not get up to give him the loaves because of their friendship, he will get up to give him whatever he needs because of his persistence.

⁹ "And I tell you, ask and you will receive; seek and you will find; knock and the door will be opened to you. ¹⁰ For everyone who asks, receives; and the one who seeks, finds; and to the one who knocks, the door will be opened. ¹¹ What father among you would hand his son a snake when he asks for a fish? ¹² Or hand him a scorpion when he asks for an egg? ¹³ If you then, who are wicked, know how to give good gifts to your children, how much more will the Father in heaven give the holy Spirit to those who ask him?"

Luke places Jesus' teaching on prayer, called by some a catechism for Gentiles, in a natural setting. Jesus' disciples, some of them once taught by the Baptist (see 5:33), ask Jesus to teach them how to pray. Undoubtedly, they noticed a connection between Jesus' powerful impact on others and his life of prayer. Throughout the Gospel Jesus deepens his close communion with God through prayer (3:21; 5:16; 6:12; 9:18, 28–29; 11:1; 22:41–45; 23:46). Without hesitation Jesus shares his own personal prayer, known to us as the "Lord's Prayer" or the "Our Father." Perhaps more than any other, this is the one prayer that all Christian groups have in common.

Unlike Matthew's version of the Lord's Prayer with its seven petitions, along with a doxology (Mt 6:9–15), Luke's rendition has five petitions. Jesus begins by addressing his prayer to Abba, "Father" (11:2; see 10:21–22). The first petition is that the Father's name be kept holy, undefiled by any evil. The holiness of God is a central theme in the Hebrew Bible, as the prophet Isaiah proclaims: "Holy, holy, holy is the LORD of hosts!" (Is 6:3). God's name is not to be taken in vain (Ex 20:7; Dt 5:11). The next petition is that the Father's kingdom may be effective in the world community. Beginning with 4:14 it has become patently clear that God's reign transcends all boundaries between the righteous and sinners, rich and poor, male and female, the clean and unclean. The arrival of God's kingdom is being proclaimed (9:2, 11, 60, 62); it is already at hand (10:9, 11).

The meaning of the third petition, "Give us each day our daily bread," is unclear. The nuance of the rare Greek word, *epiousios*, rendered by the NAB as "daily," is obscure. It is variously explained to mean: 1) sustenance food, that is, bread necessary to sustain life; 2) food for the present, thus daily bread; or 3) food for the coming day, that is, the future. Any of these meanings are possible. The first fits the context especially well, since the Twelve and the seventy-two have been sent out on mission without any food to sustain them. The present tense verb, *didou*, suggests continued action: "keep giving us." This

113

petition recalls the bountiful gift of bread at the multiplication of loaves (9:12–17).

The fourth petition about forgiveness takes up a central theme in Luke-Acts (1:77; 3:3; 5:20–24; 7:47–49; 12:10; 23:34; 24:47; Acts 2:38; 5:31; 10:43; 13:38; 26:18). The community of believers is made up of sinners in need of forgiveness for offenses against God. They in turn have also suffered from the perversity of others. The term "debts" may be understood within the community as a moral offense or in an economic sense as a loan to be forgiven. This petition recalls the connection already made in the Sermon on the Plain between forgiving and being forgiven (6:37–38).

The last petition, "Do not subject us to the final test," reflects the hard reality that like Jesus, the disciples will not be shielded from evil. They will be tested. Jesus faced temptation (4:1–13; 22:28); and so too will the disciples (8:13; 22:31, 40). In Luke's era a major test faced by some believers was that of apostasy, giving up the faith. This petition rests on the conviction that God can influence human events, a belief that Paul also expresses: "God is faithful and will not let you be tried beyond your strength" (1 Cor 10:13).

Jesus continues his teaching on prayer with two similitudes (11:5–8,11–13) given on either side of a rhythmic exhortation (11:9–10). The first is an imaginary, though true-to-life situation of a person who is out of food when a late-night guest unexpectedly arrives. So the host goes to one of his friends at midnight to ask for three loaves of bread. In the Greek world true friends are to hold all things in common, although making a request at midnight when the friend's children are all in bed is a bit of an extreme case. Even if the bonds of friendship are not enough to rouse the person from bed, he will get up because of the host's "persistence."

The second similitude is about the relationship between father and son. Jesus asks whether any father would give his son a snake or scorpion instead of fish or an egg. The answer is, of course, a resounding "no." If human parents, even those who

114

are wicked, know how to give gifts to their children, how much more will the Father give to those who ask a gift that far exceeds anything that parents can offer?

For reflection: It is true that some believers may not relate well to the image of God as Father, especially if the experience of their own human father has been less than positive. The challenge then is to allow that negative image to be transformed. For Jesus the Father is personal, caring, and gracious as well as loving, forgiving, and compassionate (see 11:10–13; 15:11–32). To focus on the paternal image for God offered here is not to overlook the many rich maternal expressions for the divine in scripture. Ultimately, of course, God is neither male nor female. Still, the use of language from familial relationships can help one to relate more closely to the Holy One.

The similitudes emphatically teach two things: first, the importance of asking for what one needs, and secondly, that whatever is asked will be granted. God is ready to respond, but believers are to do their part by asking. This does not imply that God does not already know our needs. The very act of asking is a demonstration of total dependence on the goodness of God. We are assured that the God of Jesus Christ will grant far more than what we request.

Sayings against Greed and the Parable of the Rich Fool (12:13–21)

The power of the teaching on possessions (12:31–21) and dependence on God (12:22–34) becomes all the more striking when it is read in light of the preceding context. After Jesus' teaching on prayer concluding with the promise that the Father will give the Holy Spirit to those who ask (11:13) and Jesus' expulsion of a demon (11:14), his opponents accuse him of colluding with Beelzebul, the prince of demons.

As Jesus is speaking from a crowd, a woman's voice unexpectedly praises the womb that bore him and the breasts that nursed him. Redirecting her attention, Jesus declares that those who hear the word of God and observe it are blessed (11:27–28). Then he urges the crowd to see that there is something greater here than the prophet Jonah (11:29–32). Comparing the eye of the body to a lamp, Jesus instructs the crowd to make the right choice by letting their whole body be filled with light from the word of God (11:33–36). Those who have not received the light are the Pharisees and lawyers. Jesus sternly accuses them of hypocrisy and charges that the blood of God's prophets and apostles is on their hands. The scribes and Pharisees then become increasingly hostile toward Jesus himself (11:37–54).

Not to be influenced by the hypocrisy of the Pharisees, who say one thing and act otherwise (12:1), the disciples are to show courage during times of persecution. The hostility Jesus experienced does not escape his followers. Calling them friends (12:4)—the only time this endearing term is used of the disciples in Luke—Jesus addresses their fears. He instructs them not to be afraid of their persecutors, but to fear God, who has the power to cast into Gehenna, a valley southwest of Jerusalem, considered to be a place of punishment. When the disciples are taken before synagogues, rulers, and authorities, they are not to worry about their defense, because they will be taught what to say by the Holy Spirit (12:12), who has been promised to them (11:13).

When anxieties escalate and opposition mounts, feelings of security often plummet. Grasping for some kind of protection, it is not uncommon to accumulate possessions and to hold on to them for dear life. Aware of this dynamic, Jesus unmasks the illusion that the accumulation of possessions can guarantee security.

> [13] Someone in the crowd said to him, "Teacher, tell my brother to share the inheritance with me." [14] He replied to him, "Friend, who appointed me as your judge and arbitrator?" [15]Then he said to the crowd, "Take care to guard against all greed, for though one may be rich, one's life does not consist of possessions."

116

¹⁶ Then he told them a parable. "There was a rich man whose land produced a bountiful harvest. ¹⁷He asked himself, 'What shall I do, for I do not have space to store my harvest?' ¹⁸ And he said, 'This is what I shall do: I shall tear down my barns and build larger ones. There I shall store all my grain and other goods ¹⁹ and I shall say to myself, "Now as for you, you have so many good things stored up for many years, rest, eat, drink, be merry!" ' ²⁰ But God said to him, 'You fool, this night your life will be demanded of you; and the things you have prepared, to whom will they belong?' ²¹ Thus will it be for the one who stores up treasure for himself but is not rich in what matters to God."

A massive crowd has been pressing around Jesus, trampling one another underfoot (12:1). In this frenetic fray one can imagine that some are hostile, some are accepting, and others are seeking how they can enlist Jesus to assist them. One anonymous voice insists that Jesus intervene as a lawyer to settle a family dispute over inheritance. Two siblings are evidently divided, even antagonistic over who is to inherit a desired piece of property (12:13–15; see Nm 27:1–11; 36:1–9; Dt 21:15–17). Showing no interest in the facts of the case, Jesus soundly rejects the role of judge and arbitrator. Instead, he goes straight to the heart of the matter, and addresses the covetousness that underlies the request.

Jesus instructs the whole crowd to avoid greed in all its forms and clearly teaches that a person's life does not consist of possessions. Left unchecked, greed can become like an unquenchable fire that consumes the self and erodes the soul. But rather than moralizing, Jesus tells a very unsettling parable about the attempt to equate one's life with one's possessions.

The story begins innocently enough about the good fortune of a rich man who has a bountiful harvest. A harvest is one of the positive images used for the kingdom of God, but for this rich person, the solitary figure in the picture, his great yield becomes his downfall. An interior monologue unfolds. With no place to store his bumper crop, he ponders: "What shall I do . . . ?" (12:17; see 3:10, 12, 14; 18:18). In Luke this is not a mundane query, but a question of life and death. The farmer, like a wise manager, decides to build larger grain bins to store his windfall. This seems to be a prudent decision.

His motivation, however, discloses his problem. By thus acting, he aims to provide security for the future and a relaxed lifestyle for the present, when he can eat heartily, drink well, and enjoy himself, a philosophy of life recalling Isaiah 22:13 (quoted in 1 Cor 15:32). What the rich man fails to realize is that he could die tomorrow and his stored up possessions will be of no avail.

How isolated the man is! We hear nothing about his family, friends, or even enemies. His speech betrays how closed in he is upon himself, for he does not see beyond "my crops, my barns, my gain, and my goods." He is oblivious to the socio-economic consequences of his actions, for by holding back his harvest, he deprives others and may also drive up the price of grain.

God's word of judgment shatters his sense of security. Though the farmer may consider himself to be wise, God calls him a "fool" because he is seemingly unaware of his own death and acts as if there were no God. He is a fool because he thought that he had secured his life. He has no knowledge that life is a gift or loan from God that must be returned, an idea that may be conveyed by the verb "will be demanded of" (*apaitousin*, 12:20). This man is a fool because he does not become a generous bene-factor who shares his abundance with neighbors in need, thereby transforming his possessions into never-ending heavenly capital (see 12:33). Finally, this man is a fool because he is not rich in what matters to God (12:21).

For reflection: Jesus offers much insight into the ways of the human heart. It is a natural tendency for us, aware of our own fragility and the uncertainties of life, to search for lasting security. This becomes even more pronounced when we are faced with doubts and worries, anxieties and disappointments, rejection and failure. One way of dealing with such disturbing fears is to grasp more tightly the possessions we have and to acquire even more things hoping that they will help us feel more secure about our life. Recent studies have shown that some choose to deal with depression by frequent trips to the shopping mall.

Whether a person's material possessions are few or very great, it is a temptation for everyone to place upon them ultimate value. When this happens our relationship with God easily becomes secondary, and perhaps dispensable. What are your most prized possessions? What place do they have in your life? Do you continually focus on building new grain bins by, for example, adding to a stock portfolio or increasing personal property? In what ways do you need a conversion of heart so that you can become a more generous benefactor sharing your possessions with those in need?

Dependence on God (12:22–34)

²² He said to [his] disciples, "Therefore I tell you, do not worry about your life and what you will eat, or about your body and what you will wear. ²³ For life is more than food and the body more than clothing. ²⁴ Notice the ravens: they do not sow or reap; they have neither storehouse nor barn, yet God feeds them. How much more important are you than birds! ²⁵ Can any of you by worrying add a moment to your lifespan? ²⁶ If even the smallest things are beyond your control, why are you anxious about the rest? ²⁷ Notice how the flowers grow. They do not toil or spin. But I tell you, not even Solomon in all his splendor was dressed like one of them. ²⁸ If God so clothes the grass in the field that grows today and is thrown into the oven tomorrow, will he not much more provide for you, O you of little faith? ²⁹ As for you, do not seek what you are to eat and what you are to drink, and do not worry anymore. ³⁰ All the nations of the world seek for these things, and your Father knows that you need them. ³¹ Instead, seek

his kingdom, and these other things will be given you besides. ³² Do not be afraid any longer, little flock, for your Father is pleased to give you the kingdom. ³³ Sell your belongings and give alms. Provide money bags for yourselves that do not wear out, an inexhaustible treasure in heaven that no thief can reach nor moth destroy. ³⁴ For where your treasure is, there also will your heart be."

After addressing the crowds, Jesus turns his attention to the disciples. Since they are near the opposite end of the economic ladder from the rich man, and have already left behind everything (5:11; 28), it is understandable that they fret about their life, whether they would have food to eat or clothes to wear. In response Jesus again tells them not to worry (12:22–23, see 12:6–7). He offers two comparisons, one with the birds and the other with the flowers, parallels that cannot be dismissed as romantic idealism.

Rather than choosing robust examples of strong lions or towering cedars of Lebanon, Jesus brings his disciples' attention first to ravens. Ravens are unclean birds (Lv 11:15; Dt 14:14), known as careless creatures who can get lost returning to their nests. Ravens neither reap nor sow, have neither storehouses or barns, yet God provides for them. Arguing from the lesser to the greater, Jesus affirms how much more important his disciples are than these birds. So why worry?

Even stronger language is used in the second comparison. This time Jesus invites his disciples to imagine how flowers, usually translated as lilies, grow. Without any effort or toil on their part, they have a splendor that is even far greater than that of Solomon, the most powerful king of Jewish antiquity. God cares for these flowers even though their beauty is fleeting and they are thrown in the fire tomorrow. If God provides in such a way for the lilies, how much more will God provide for you? Jesus directs his readers' imaginations to situations when their lives seem as helpless and fleeting as lowly ravens and ephemeral flowers. Chiding them for their little faith, Jesus counsels his disciples to worry no longer, for God provides for them.

Changing to more endearing language, Jesus reminds his disciples that they have a Father who knows what they need. Jesus continues in this vein and refers to them with the gentle image of "little flock," recalling the tender way that God cared for Israel of old (Ez 34:11–24). They no longer need to be afraid because the kingdom has been given to them. The kingdom they have been encouraged to seek (12:31) is available to them as a gift from the Father (12:32).

This section concludes with a categorical command: "Sell your belongings and give alms" (12:33). This applies not so much to the disciples of Jesus who have already left behind everything, but to the believers in Luke's community who would have possessions. The verb "sell" emphasizes that substantial personal property is to be sold, and not just spare money given to the destitute. Those with possessions are to sell these and give alms. The word "almsgiving" comes from the Greek *eleēmosunē*, originally meaning compassion or fellow feeling, and then gift. The compassion that evoked the act of giving has become the name for the act itself. To give alms not only benefits those in need but also creates bonds of community between the haves and the have-nots. By disposing of their own possessions, the well-off can begin to share in some of the same risks and thus have the same trust as the destitute who are forced to rely upon the Father alone.

The reason for giving alms is to build up an inexhaustible treasure in heaven. In this process material wealth becomes a means for showing mercy and thus is exchanged for a wealth that is secure. Those who once invested their hearts in earthly treasures are called to invest their hearts in God. "For," as Jesus says, "where your treasure is, there also will your heart be" (12:34).

For reflection: How easy it is for worry to dominate one's daily life. The claim can easily be made that a worrier has many valid reasons to be preoccupied by anxious thoughts. Jesus directly challenges this way of being. A mind stuck in the worry track can hardly be open to God's providential ways. Sometimes, this practical advice has been given to one who keeps revisiting troubling thoughts: set aside five minutes a day to worry, and after that get on with the day knowing that the same God who provides for the birds of the air and the splendor of the flowers cares so much more for us, God's friends and the Father's little flock.

Jesus draws our imaginations into a rich encounter with the goodness and beauty of creation. The splendor of God's handiwork was there long before we came upon the face of the earth, and will be there long after we die, that is, if it does not become too tarnished by unmitigated "development" and ecological neglect. Slowing down enough to behold the magnificence of nature around us can dissipate our worries and remind us to trust the Creator more fully.

The kingdom of God has indeed been given to us. Our call is to proclaim this kingdom by the way we deal with our possessions. Not by holding on to them with the illusion that they will guarantee our life and protect us from harm on the outside and worry on the inside, but by sharing these generously with those around us will we provide a lasting treasure in heaven. This passage awakens us to adopt a counter-cultural perspective on possessions and to act accordingly.

A Call to Repentance (13:1–9)

The call for repentance in 13:1–9 follows a poignant parable and several sayings from Jesus about the need to change behavior and act now while there is still time before the Son of Man returns (12:40, 46; see 12:20). The servant parables (12:35–48) are told at a time that reflects a decreased intensity regarding the imminent return of the Messiah. In the earliest

New Testament document, First Thessalonians, Paul's view and that of the new believers in the Greek city of Thessalonica, is that the Lord was expected to return at any moment. This intense expectation created a crisis of belief when some of their number died before the anticipated return of the Lord (1 Thes 4:13–18). By the time of Luke's Gospel this expectation had waned. Nonetheless, Jesus warns the faithful not to view the Lord's return as such a remote event that it should no longer be a concern.

The master of the house in the first parable (12:35–40) represents the Lord who will return at an unexpected moment, and the servants and steward are those who served the Christian community in leadership positions. Although Jesus does not directly answer Peter's question as to whether the parable is meant "for us or for everyone" (12:41), Jesus' response suggests a particular application to those in leadership positions in the early church (12:39, 42–48). The reference to the abusive and complacent servant/church official who beats the servants under him and who eats, drinks and gets drunk (12:45) recalls the rich man whom God has called a fool for planning to do the same thing (12:19). By contrast, those servants who faithfully carry out the mission of Jesus are called blessed (12:37, 38, 43).

Jesus' message may be very disturbing to families, causing conflict and bringing division between those members who accept him and those who do not (12:49–53; cf. 8:19–21; 9:59–62; 14:26; 18:28–30). As a flashback to the Baptist's preaching (3:16), the fire that Jesus brings is an urgent call for purification (12:49). The baptism that Jesus will experience is not to be understood merely as a water ritual but serves as a symbol for his own death.

In response to a questioner, Jesus warns the crowds to use their weather predicting skills to interpret the signs of the present (12:54–56), to recognize that he is accomplishing God's work of salvation, and to take action (12:57–59). This leads up to an urgent call to repentance.

^{13:1} At that time some people who were present there told him about the Galileans whose blood Pilate had mingled with the blood of their sacrifices. ² He said to them in reply, "Do you think that because these Galileans suffered in this way they were greater sinners than all other Galileans? ³ By no means! But I tell you, if you do not repent, you will all perish as they did! ⁴ Or those eighteen people who were killed when the tower at Siloam fell on them—do you think they were more guilty than everyone else who lived in Jerusalem? ⁵ By no means! But I tell you, if you do not repent, you will all perish as they did!"

⁶ And he told them this parable: "There once was a person who had a fig tree planted in his orchard, and when he came in search of fruit on it but found none, ⁷ he said to the gardener, 'For three years now I have come in search of fruit on this fig tree but have found none. [So] cut it down. Why should it exhaust the soil?' ⁸ He said to him in reply, 'Sir, leave it for this year also, and I shall cultivate the ground around it and fertilize it; ⁹ it may bear fruit in the future. If not you can cut it down.' "

This passage refers to two reports about multiple deaths that are not recounted in any other source outside the New Testament. The slaughter of Galileans by Pilate fits with the character of this ruler. The Jewish historian Josephus reports that on one occasion Pilate killed a number of Samaritans gathered at Mt. Gerizim and on another occasion put to death some Jews who objected when Pilate took money from the Temple. As atrocious as the Galilean incident must have been, Jesus does not respond to this report by calling for vengeance against the perpetrator.

Using a rhetorical question requiring "no" for an answer, Jesus insists that these unfortunate Galileans are not to be seen as notorious sinners because they were put to death. Instead, Jesus calls for repentance, warning that those who do not change heart will perish. Then citing a second catastrophe, the death of eighteen people upon whom the tower of Siloam fell, Jesus emphatically reiterates the same call to repent.

The lesson drawn from these two reported disasters is clear. The crowds and the disciples are to repent while there is still time. The purpose of these catastrophes is not to instill fear, but to get the attention of those who may be like the lackadaisical servants of the previous parable (12:35–48). Conversion of heart and acceptance of God's prophet are required now before it is too late. Unexpected death can come to anyone.

The accompanying parable of the fig tree is also intended to light a fire under would be procrastinators. The owner of the fig tree expresses indignation to his gardener because this tree has borne no fruit for three years. He demands that it be removed. Not ready to give up hope yet, the gardener asks for another year to cultivate and fertilize it. Evidently, his plea is successful. More time is given, but not an indefinite period. The application is clear. Those in the crowd around Jesus—and those in Luke's community—are given a grace period to repent and bear fruit. The delay will not, however, be permanent.

For reflection: Believers today certainly live with a very different outlook on the return of the Messiah or the end of the world than was held during Jesus' generation. Except for the over-zealous expectation of a few at the close of the Second Millennium who thought that this might be it, for most the end hardly enters our consciousness.

Where does this leave disciples of Jesus at the dawn of the third millennium? The counsel of many, to live each day as if it were one's last, contains much wisdom. Ignatius of Loyola in the *Spiritual Exercises* offers this advice: consider what the choices made today will look like "as if I were at the point of death." Similarly, the *Imitation of Christ* recommends that "every action of yours, every thought, should be those of one who expects to die before the day is out."

It is a noble intention to live and act in a way that always advances God's reign. Certainly this passage is an urgent call to become reconciled to God and to one another. Who are those in your family, among your friends, or in your community with whom you need to make peace? And, are there areas of your life that are still closed off from relationship with God? What steps do you need to take today to live in peace and harmony? Finally, what thoughts and feelings come up when you consider your mortality? Reflecting on our own death can prompt us to re-evaluate priorities, to make changes, and thus to become more faithful disciples of Jesus.

Cure of a Crippled Woman on the Sabbath and Two Kingdom Parables (13:10–20)

[10] He was teaching in a synagogue on the sabbath. [11] And a woman was there who for eighteen years had been crippled by a spirit; she was bent over, completely incapable of standing erect. [12] When Jesus saw her, he called to her and said, "Woman, you are set free of your infirmity." [13] He laid his hands on her, and she at once stood up straight and glorified God. [14] But the leader of the synagogue, indignant that Jesus had cured on the sabbath, said to the crowd in reply, "There are six days when work should be done. Come on those days to be cured, not on the sabbath day." [15] The Lord said to him in reply, "Hypocrites! Does not each one of you on the sabbath untie his ox or his ass from the manger and lead it out for watering? [16] This daughter of Abraham, whom Satan has bound for eighteen years now, ought she not to have been set free on the sabbath day from this bondage?" [17] When he said this, all his adversaries were humiliated; and the whole crowd rejoiced at all the splendid deeds done by him.

[18] Then he said, "What is the kingdom of God like? To what can I compare it? [19] It is like a mustard seed that a person took and planted in the garden. When it was fully grown, it became a large bush and 'the birds of the sky dwelt in its branches.' "

[20] Again he said, "To what shall I compare the kingdom of God? [21] It is like yeast that a woman took and mixed [in] with

three measures of wheat flour until the whole batch of dough was leavened."

While teaching in a synagogue on the sabbath, Jesus notices a woman who has for eighteen years been crippled by a spirit (literally: "spirit of weakness"). Similar to the woman with the hemorrhage (8:43–48), this woman would have lived on the margins of society. Today, it might be said that she suffered from osteoporosis, whereas in first century Palestine illnesses were often attributed to some kind of evil spirit (see 4:33, 36; 6:18; 7:21; 8:2, 29; 9:42). Jesus responds to her need by touching her—breaking the boundaries of isolation she may have felt—to set her free from her infirmity. Later in the travel narrative, Jesus will cure a man with dropsy on the sabbath (14:1–6), reflecting Luke's pattern of featuring both men and women in juxtaposition (see also 7:11–17/8:49–56 and 13:10–17/14:1–6). God's kingdom does not give preference to one gender over another.

The synagogue leader became indignant because Jesus was breaking the sabbath. Whether this leader would have been more open to the cure had the one in need of healing been a man, there is no way of knowing. Assuming that the crowd was sympathetic to Jesus' action, the synagogue leader addressed the crowd by citing the sabbath commandment probably hoping to win them over to his side.

In a quick repartee Jesus called this religious leader and those like him hypocrites. Then Jesus persuasively argues his case by making a lesser-to-greater comparison. If the Law allows one to untie an ox or donkey for watering on the sabbath, how much more ought it to permit a bent over woman to be freed from Satan's bondage. Jesus' argument implies two contrasts: the first is that this woman is worth far more than a beast of burden, and secondly, the brief wait that animals have before being watered pales in significance to the eighteen years that this crippled woman waited to be healed.

Jesus underscores the woman's dignity by calling her a daughter of Abraham. This is her rightful heritage and no long term infirmity is to deprive her of it—contrary to what others might think. Later Jesus will also name Zacchaeus, a sinner and a tax collector, a "descendant of Abraham" (19:9). Echoing the stance taken by John the Baptist, Jesus does not limit membership in the family of Abraham to narrowly defined boundaries, but includes among reconstituted Israel all those—the infirm, the sinners, and the outcast—who accept God's prophet.

In freeing this woman and answering his critics, Jesus humbles the opposition—actually, their narrow, legalistic views brought humiliation on themselves. The whole crowd, however, rejoiced at all the splendid deeds Jesus worked, suggesting that this was just one among many.

The two following brief parables about the Kingdom are directly linked to the healing of the woman. They illustrate that God's reign grows regardless of opposition (see 13:10–17; see 14:1–24). A mustard seed, known to be the smallest of seeds—a commonly accepted observation, though not mentioned by Luke—is planted and becomes a tree (literal translation). Actually, mustard seeds became hard-to-control bushes, thus the NAB translation, "large bush." In this "tree" birds of the sky dwell (see Ps 104:12; Ez 17:22–23; 31:3–6; Dn 4:9,10–12, 18). The assumption is that all kinds of birds come to rest, thus reflecting the diversity of people who find refuge in the kingdom.

In a second example, Jesus compares the kingdom of God to yeast (literally, "leaven") that is put into a large amount of wheat flour. Three measures is about thirty-six quarts or one bushel. That little bit of leaven causes the whole batch of dough to rise. To understand the force of this comparison it is helpful to recall that leaven comes from bread that is allowed to rot, and thus it is a symbol of corruption, or of that which is unclean (see the negative use of this in 12:1). A second factor is that the leaven is hidden in a large amount of dough.

Taking both of these parables together, Jesus emphasizes that the kingdom will grow regardless of opposition from synagogue leaders, Pharisees, or scholars of the law. From small, even hidden beginnings it will become a significant reality where all kinds of people can find a place, even the crippled woman who was healed on the sabbath. Like the leaven, God's reign will permeate the whole.

For reflection: Rules and regulations, even religious ones, can and do play an important function in establishing a harmonious life among the members of a believing community. They help to draw boundaries, to identify rights and responsibilities, and to clarify roles. However, it is also possible that rules can be used in a way similar to what the synagogue leader did with the sabbath regulation, that is, to keep people in bondage. When this happens ecclesiastical canons need to be revisited by church leadership. From this healing story a guiding principle is for the church to establish rules and guidelines that assist the believing community in freeing those in bondage.

A second reflection pertains to the pastoral care of the sick. Many who are suffering from illness, whether this be cancer, AIDS, arthritis, or Parkinson's, can easily feel isolated from family members, friends and the faith community. Illness tends to create boundaries between the well and the infirm. One of the most caring responses is certainly to be present to those who are ill, and also, in appropriate ways to hold the person's hand, to give a hug, or simply to touch the person. More healing can come from a loving touch than a thousand words. To touch with compassion is a way of reassuring the sick person that he or she is still very much part of the community.

V

The Journey to Jerusalem Continues
(13:22–17:10)

Jesus continues to teach and to heal as he makes his way toward Jerusalem (13:22), for that is the city where the prophet must die (13:33). A healing (14:1–6) and two parables (14:7–14; 15–24) take place at table. The parables present a view of those invited to the kingdom that far surpasses the boundaries of conventional expectations. Those called to discipleship are again reminded about the necessity to take up the cross, to count the cost, and to be prepared to renounce all possessions for the sake of the kingdom (14:25–33).

Emphasizing that those invited to the kingdom include the lost and the forsaken, tax collectors and sinners, Jesus tells three parables about the need for repentance and the abundance of God's mercy (15:1–7, 8–10, 11–32). Through additional parables and sayings Jesus teaches about the prudent use of material resources (16:1–13), warns against the love of money (16:14–15), and express God's attitude toward the rich and the poor (16:19–31).

This section continues with Jesus instructing the disciples about temptations to sin (17:1–4), the necessity to have faith (17:5–6), and the importance of doing what they have been called to do as servants of the kingdom (17:7–10).

Acceptance and Rejection of Salvation (13:22–35)

²² He passed through towns and villages, teaching as he went and making his way to Jerusalem. ²³ Someone asked him, "Lord, will only a few people be saved?" He answered

them, ²⁴"Strive to enter through the narrow gate, for many, I tell you, will attempt to enter but will not be strong enough. ²⁵ After the master of the house has arisen and locked the door, then will you stand outside knocking and saying, 'Lord, open the door for us.' He will say to you in reply, 'I do not know where you are from.' ²⁶ And you will say, 'We ate and drank in your company and you taught in our streets.' ²⁷Then he will say to you, 'I do not know where [you] are from. Depart from me, all you evildoers!' ²⁸ And there will be wailing and grinding of teeth when you see Abraham, Isaac, and Jacob and all the prophets in the kingdom of God and you yourselves cast out. ²⁹And people will come from the east and the west and from the north and the south and will recline at table in the kingdom of God. ³⁰For behold, some are last who will be first, and some are first who will be last."

³¹ At that time some Pharisees came to him and said, "Go away, leave this area because Herod wants to kill you." ³² He replied, "Go and tell that fox, 'Behold, I cast out demons and I perform healings today and tomorrow, and on the third day I accomplish my purpose. ³³ Yet I must continue on my way today, tomorrow, and the following day, for it is impossible that a prophet should die outside of Jerusalem.'

³⁴ "Jerusalem, Jerusalem, you who kill the prophets and stone those sent to you, how many times I yearned to gather your children together as a hen gathers her brood under her wings, but you were unwilling! ³⁵ Behold, your house will be abandoned. (But) I tell you, you will not see me until (the time comes when) you say, 'Blessed is he who comes in the name of the Lord.' "

This passage vividly reminds us that Jesus is on a journey to Jerusalem (13:22), the city where the prophets were killed (13:34), and where he himself must die (13:33). Passing through towns and villages Jesus continues to teach as he resolutely heads for the city of his destination. An anonymous questioner, who reminds us that crowds continually accompany Jesus, asks whether a few will be saved. In response Jesus directs his hearers to enter through the narrow opening rather than through the large city gates. The stress here is not that few will be saved but that many will not be able (that is, not be strong enough) to enter because they have not shown the fruits of repentance (see 13:3, 5).

The narrow gate will not be open indefinitely, for the master of the house will rise and lock the door—notice the change of image from gate to door—on those content with boasting. The Greek verb *egeirō,* here meaning "has arisen" (13:25), is the same as that used for the resurrection of Jesus, suggesting that we are to read this as an allegory in which the master represents Jesus. Some will realize too late what is required of them, and they will be excluded. Even though they will claim to have dined with Jesus and to have noticed him teaching in their streets, this is not sufficient. Casual acquaintance does not gain entrance into the kingdom or an invitation to the heavenly banquet. Some religious leaders of Jesus' time can certainly claim to have dined with Jesus, but this in itself had little effect since they were not receptive to him or to his message.

Using harsh language the master of the house calls those on the outside evildoers (13:27, see Ps 6:9). They will experience wailing and grinding of teeth, a graphic image of final judgment and condemnation. Exacerbating their sense of exclusion, those cast out will be aware that their forefathers and the prophets will be at the banquet for faithful Israel. Thus, the promises made in ages past to Abraham, Isaac, and Jacob will be fulfilled.

Not limited to a select few (see 13:23), God's eschatological banquet will be opened to all peoples, a theme to be underscored in 14:15–24. The four cardinal directions (13:29), a symbol of universality, suggests that people will come from all over the globe, including Gentiles and Jews from the diaspora. This fulfills the Scriptural promises made long ago about the regathering of scattered Israel (see Ps 107:2–3; Is 11:11–12; 43:5–6). This also anticipates the Pentecost event when Peter addresses those from many lands (Acts 2:5–11). Together these people will form reconstituted Israel.

Seeking to deter Jesus from his intended itinerary, some Pharisees warn Jesus about Herod Antipas' intent to kill him (13:31). If their motif was Jesus' safety, this would be Luke's only positive reference to the Pharisees in his Gospel. If not, does their warning reflect a hostile effort to get Jesus out of the territory? Whatever the case, Herod remains a serious threat, for he beheaded John the Baptist. Notwithstanding Herod's animosity, Jesus remains resolute in his determination to fulfill God's will by establishing the kingdom. The reference to the third day evokes for the reader the resurrection, God's ultimate vindication of Jesus (13:32).

In an emotionally laden lament anticipating 19:41–44, Jesus addresses personified Jerusalem and indicts that city of peace (the literal meaning of Jerusalem) for the role it played in killing the prophets (13:34). Then, Jesus dramatically changes the tone by comparing his aspiration to that of a hen who would gather its chicks under the protective care of its wings. This maternal image, rich in caring compassion, conveys Jesus' desire to shelter the inhabitants of this city from its own iniquity. However, his yearning finds no response, for the people were unwilling to accept him.

As pessimistic as this lament sounds, the Lukan Jesus concludes with a theme of hope, referring to a time in the future when his followers will see him again and greet him with: "Blessed is he who comes in the name of the Lord." This expression, used by pilgrims when they enter Jerusalem for festivals, is the same greeting that is announced when Jesus goes into that city (19:38; see Ps 118:26). Jesus' prophetic announcement declares that he will not return to Jerusalem until it is ready to welcome him for who he is, God's Messiah.

For reflection: The Christian way of life is not for those who are inclined to take the path of least resistance. Even association with committed believers or familiarity with the teachings of the Master, while helpful, in no way offers assurance to those seeking to dine at the banquet in the kingdom. Whatever spiritual credentials a person might claim—even writing a commentary on the Gospel of Luke!—will be of no avail unless that person experiences a genuine conversion to live out Gospel values.

Coming at the end of this passage about weeping and grinding of teeth, about evildoers and the killing of prophets, there is a very warm, maternal image of Jesus. With tender care Jesus longs to gather all those who are so inclined to find shelter under his protective wing. This image is particularly consoling to those in special need of comfort, love and mercy. Who has not been in this space at one time or another? Although little emphasized in Christian tradition, the maternal image of Jesus plays an important place in spiritual writings. For example, Juliana of Norwich, in *The Cloud of Unknowing*, refers to Jesus as "our Mother of mercy," thus capturing the nurturing presence that Jesus offers.

In a quiet moment, recall whether you have encountered the presence of Jesus as a nurturing mother. If so, what was this like and how did the experience nourish your spiritual life? If not, this passage reminds us to be open to the feminine side of the Divine Lover, and to cherish these experiences when they come our way.

Conduct of Invited Guests and which Guests to Invite (Lk 14:7–14)

As he regularly does, Jesus dines at the home of one of the leading Pharisees (7:36–50; 11:37–54). This banquet becomes the setting for Jesus' teaching about the expected conduct of invited guests (14:7–11), about who should be invited (14:12–14), and finally, about the kingdom of God metaphorically presented as a dinner party (14:15–24). Having the means to host a banquet this Pharisaic leader functions as a representative of those with status and economic resources, for example, those in Luke's community who are similarly well placed.

At this sabbath dinner an uninvited guest unexpectedly shows up, a man with dropsy (14:1–6). Soon we will learn that this is the kind of person whom the Pharisee should have invited but did not. The afflicted man's medical condition—referred to today as edema—involves the abnormal swelling of the body due to the retention of excess fluid. As in previous sabbath healings, Jesus dominates the scene by asking his adversaries questions that they do not or cannot answer (6:6–11; 13:10–17). Unfazed by the cold silence of the invited guests, Jesus took the man and healed him. Jesus then uses the occasion to tell a parable about proper seating conduct for dinner guests.

⁷He told a parable to those who had been invited, noticing how they were choosing the places of honor at the table. ⁸ "When you are invited by someone to a wedding banquet, do not recline at table in the place of honor. A more distinguished guest than you may have been invited by him, ⁹ and the host who invited both of you may approach you and say, 'Give your place to this man,' and then you would proceed with embarrassment to take the lowest place. ¹⁰Rather, when you are invited, go and take the lowest place so that when the host comes to you he may say, 'My friend, move up to a higher position.' Then you will enjoy the esteem of your companions at the table. ¹¹For everyone who exalts himself will be humbled, but the one who humbles himself will be exalted." ¹²Then he said to the host who invited him, "When you hold a lunch or a dinner, do not invite your friends or your brothers or your relatives or your wealthy neighbors, in case they may invite you back and you have repayment. ¹³Rather, when you hold a banquet, invite the poor, the crippled, the lame, the blind; ¹⁴blessed indeed will you be because of their inability to repay you. For you will be repaid at the resurrection of the righteous."

Noticing the self-promoting behavior of his fellow guests who seek out places of honor, Jesus instructs them about the perils of being first. The term *prōtoklisia*, translated "places of honor," literally means "first couch." At this time it was customary for couches to be arranged in order with the first reserved for the highest ranking and most esteemed guests. In a metaphorical sense to choose the first couch refers to those whose ambition is to attain the highest social status. Jesus names this behavior and warns of embarrassing social consequences (14:9), but even more, of a reversal of fortunes at the eschatological banquet of God's kingdom (14:11).

In a previous discourse at a banquet Jesus has already come down hard on the Pharisees because they "love the seat of honor in synagogues" (11:43; see 16:15; 20:46). Jesus proclaims to their surprise that God will turn the tables: "For everyone who exalts himself will be humbled, but the one who humbles himself will be exalted" (14:11). Implied in the future passive tense, "will be," is the decisive action of God. Not only does this proverbial saying reflect secular wisdom, it also affirms how God views human behavior: the self-important will be humbled and the humbled will be raised up!

There is a common structural pattern that closely links this parable (14:7–11) to the following three verses (14:12–14). Jesus gives two examples of human behavior. First, he describes the circumstance ("when you . . . "), then gives a negative command ("do not . . . "), followed by the consequence. Secondly, Jesus presents the same situation again, but this time gives a positive command and the rationale. Thus the pattern is: "When you . . . negative command . . . consequence . . . " (14:8–9) and then "when you . . . positive command . . . rationale . . . " (14:10–11). This pattern is repeated in 14:12–14. Jesus' argument is straightforward. In the eyes of God not all behavior is commendable or praiseworthy. Using seating choices at dinner as an example, Jesus instructs his guests that God is not impressed by self-promoting behavior.

Jesus continues to address the issue of social status as he moves to a discussion of who should be invited (14:12–14). When drawing up a guest list, the common practice within

Greco-Roman society was for the host to invite friends, brothers, relatives, and wealthy neighbors. The underlying ethic was one of balanced reciprocity. By only asking friends, family, or the elite, the host maintains his status as an honored member of society. The unspoken expectation is that those invited would have the means to return the invitation, thereby acknowledging the elite status of the host who first extended hospitality at his dinner table. The initial host can expect to be invited and thus to be fully repaid.

Jesus offers a radically new instruction to all hosts. Invite those who cannot return the favor: ask the poor, the maimed, the lame, and the blind. These are overlapping social groups on the fringes of society. The poor are those who are live in material poverty and are homeless. The sick, unable to work and hence without resources like the man with dropsy, are also among the poor. But the host who extends hospitality to these outsiders risks being dishonored by family and well-placed friends.

Though such gracious action may be scorned by the elite, these hosts will be among the righteous who will be repaid at the resurrection. It is compelling that Jesus, in the presence of a leading Pharisee, promises the resurrection, a central tenet of the Pharisees (Acts 23:6–8), as the reward to those who host guests from the very bottom of the social pyramid. Jesus introduces this reward as a beatitude: "Blessed indeed will you be . . ." thus announcing to the affluent that there is a way for them to be rewarded. This stands in positive contrast to the warning of woes that had been directed to the rich in the Sermon on the Plain (6:24–25). There is indeed a way for the rich to be pronounced blessed, and that is for them to so identify with the poor that they invite them to dine in their homes. There is a reciprocity at play, but that happens on a theological rather than sociological plane. The reciprocity that counts is in the hands of God, not in the actions of the social elites.

Retrospectively, the short section of 14:12–14 sheds light on 14:11. Those who invite friends and family are the ones who exalt themselves; whereas those who host the poor, the crippled and the blind humble themselves. In God's kingdom their fortunes will be reversed.

For reflection: On a regular basis believers are faced with two choices, one which has a negative consequence and the other with a positive benefit. Before acting, it is helpful to review the choices before us, and to reflect upon these in light of Gospel values. It is easy for our action to be determined by the mores of the dominant culture. In the eyes of Jesus whoever promotes oneself or acts expecting repayment from others in a *quid pro quo* arrangement is far from living out the values of the kingdom.

How many of my daily actions are determined by an effort to make myself look good in others' eyes? How much of my time and energy is devoted to promote my career, my status, my place in the world? This passage prompts us to pause and to re-evaluate. Is there a true north to my moral compass, or does it point in whatever direction I can attain the greatest personal benefit?

The Parable of the Great Feast (Lk 14:15–24)

[15] One of his fellow guests on hearing this said to him, "Blessed is the one who will dine in the kingdom of God." [16] He replied to him, "A man gave a great dinner to which he invited many. [17] When the time for the dinner came, he dispatched his servant to say to those invited, 'Come, everything is now ready.' [18] But one by one, they all began to excuse themselves. The first said to him, 'I have purchased a field and must go to examine it; I ask you, consider me excused.' [19] And another said, 'I have purchased five yoke of oxen and am on my way to evaluate them; I ask you, consider me excused.' [20] And another said, 'I have just married a woman, and therefore I cannot come.' [21] The servant went and reported this to his master. Then the master of the house in a rage commanded his servant, 'Go out quickly into the streets

and alleys of the town and bring in here the poor and the crippled, the blind and the lame.' [22] The servant reported, 'Sir, your orders have been carried out and still there is room.' [23] The master then ordered the servant, 'Go out to the highways and hedgerows and make people come in that my home may be filled. [24] For, I tell you, none of those men who were invited will taste my dinner.' "

The parable of the Great Dinner is a good news/bad news story. It is bad news for those who declined the invitation because they had other, more pressing concerns. It is very good news to those who were invited to take their place. The beatitude just proclaimed by Jesus (14:14) prompts a member of the Pharisee's dinner party to correct Jesus by offering his version: "Blessed is the one who will dine in the kingdom of God" (14:15). This shifts the focus from banquets hosted by humans in the previous story to the eschatological banquet. This dinner guest seems to be saying that it is not those who invited the poor, the lame, and the blind who are blessed, but anyone who actually shares in the banquet of the kingdom. Not specifically rejecting the beatitude by the self-assured guest, Jesus tells another parable that discloses an unexpected reversal. The anticipated invitees will not be there; the initially uninvited will take their place.

This second banquet parable emphasizes the consequences of those who fail to respond and underscores the good fortune of those who do. This story begins by presenting a person wealthy enough to host a large dinner for guests who are well situated economically. The narrative unfolds in sets of threes. We hear about three who were initially invited to the banquet, three excuses, and three sendings of the servant (14:17–24). The first invitee could afford to buy ten oxen, another to purchase a field, and a third is busy with his new wife. All make last minute excuses, the first two because they are pursing mammon, and the last because of the demands of domestic life.

Usually one would welcome such a banquet invitation because of the honor extended to the invitees, but this social benefit does not prevail. Those invited were more engrossed in their own pursuits than in the Lord's call. With his own honor at stake by the social affront of those who refused to attend, the master of the banquet became angry and sent out his servant again. This time the servant is instructed to go to those at the bottom of the social hierarchy, the poor, the crippled, the lame, and the blind. These are the same ones who have been the beneficiaries of the healings and good news proclaimed by Jesus (7:22). Yet even these do not fill the tables at the wedding feast.

A third invitation has the servant going out to the highways and hedgerows. Unaccustomed to being invited guests, these marginalized have to be gently persuaded to enter for the festive dinner. This last group may well refer to the Gentiles, those outside the city walls. They, too, are invited for the master's home must be filled. As in an earlier parable, people from every corner are invited to recline at the banquet (see 13:29).

There are two sets of framing verses that help us to understand this parable. Verse 15 clearly indicates that this wedding feast is actually about the banquet in God's kingdom. Verse 24 declares in a absolute way that none of those initially invited will have a place at the heavenly banquet. This serves as a sound warning to all those dining with Jesus, especially to the Pharisees and lawyers who reject God's prophet. In not accepting the invitation they themselves are in danger of being excluded from the banquet. This recalls similar warnings that have been made to the non-responsive crowd (11:29–32; 12:54–13:9; 13:23–30). Hearing the words of Jesus and eating with him are no guarantee of a place at the eschatological banquet.

A larger interpretive frame is provided by the surrounding passages (14:12–14 and 14:25–33). The master of the wedding feast is a positive example of 14:13, and hence is to be commended, for he did call upon the disenfranchised (14:21). And looking ahead to the following passage, the inviting host exemplifies the action of a disciple who considers the costs of discipleship (14:25–32), follows through with his plan, and uses his resources to invite the poor and marginalized (14:33). Like this host, the rich and propertied members of Luke's community were challenged to extend hospitality to the poor, to treat these as friends at the table.

For reflection: This parable is a sober reminder to all those who believe that they will have a privileged place in the kingdom, either because of church work, religious office, or spiritual benefits. The message is especially poignant for those who have responded by working with the poor either through social service agencies or soup kitchens. Such service is indeed laudable. Yet it is an arresting thought that the very ones who are served, the poor, are those who will be invited to God's banquet. What do the poor teach us about God's invitation?

Our God is a very gracious God. The non-elect according to human standards are those specially selected by the Father to be at the heavenly banquet table. They will be the recipients of divine favor and hospitality.

Many seem to have good reasons for declining the dinner invitation. Concern for material things or domestic relationships do make their demands on the disciples of Jesus. What obstacles do you face in responding to the banquet invitation?

Sayings on Discipleship (Lk 14:25–35)

²⁵ Great crowds were traveling with him, and he turned and addressed them, ²⁶ "If anyone comes to me without hating his father and mother, wife and children, brothers and sisters, and even his own life, he cannot be my disciple. ²⁷ Whoever does not carry his own cross and come after me cannot be my disciple. ²⁸ Which of you wishing to construct a tower does not first sit down and calculate the cost to see if there is enough for its completion? ²⁹ Otherwise, after laying the foundation and finding himself unable to finish the work the onlookers should laugh at him ³⁰ and say, 'This one began to

build but did not have the resources to finish.' [31] Or what king marching into battle would not first sit down and decide whether with ten thousand troops he can successfully oppose another king advancing upon him with twenty thousand troops? [32] But if not, while he is still far away, he will send a delegation to ask for peace terms. [33] In the same way, everyone of you who does not renounce all his possessions cannot be my disciple.

[34] "Salt is good, but if salt itself loses its taste, with what can its flavor be restored? [35] It is fit neither for the soil nor for the manure pile; it is thrown out. Whoever has ears to hear ought to hear."

The focus shifts from God's gracious action in the previous parable to the radical demands on a disciple. Jesus has already stated the requirements for following him (9:23–27, 57–62). In this passage the language is even sharper and more shocking. There are a series of three challenges to discipleship requiring drastic action (14:26, 27, 33), followed by the negative consequence: " . . . cannot be my disciple." The person who does not hate family members, take up the cross, or renounce all possessions, cannot be a follower of Jesus. It is a wonder that the great crowds following Jesus did not leave him in large numbers after hearing such seemingly impossible demands.

In light of the threats today to the integrity of the family brought about by a high incidence of divorce, the first absolute conditional sentence—"If anyone comes to me without hating family members"—seems to be the opposite of what we might expect Jesus to require. The verb "hate" is not to be understood so much as an emotional response, but rather as parabolic language that stresses the radical call of discipleship. Here hate means to leave old loyalties behind. Choosing Jesus means to let go of all relationships that hinder in any way the new life of a disciple.

Family is to take second place behind the demands of the kingdom. Luke has a number of sayings that reflect a harsh attitude to family loyalties that impede becoming a disciple (8:19–21; 9:59–62; 12:51–53; 18:29; 21:16). In the previous passage domestic responsibilities to his wife kept one young man from participating in the banquet. That single example of domestic hindrance is now globalized in this requirement. Neither father, mother, wife (husband is not mentioned), children, brothers, sisters, or even one's own life is to be preferred over the disciple's relationship to Jesus.

The final loyalty to be rejected, "even one's own life," suggests that martyrdom itself may be required. This meaning is reinforced by the next requirement to carry the cross. Personal safety is to be sacrificed, and suffering is to be accepted as the cost for following Jesus on the journey.

Before the requirement about possessions, two brief parables emphasize the need to carefully count the cost before embarking on the journey. The builder who cannot complete the tower he set out to construct will be ridiculed. The king who encounters in battle a larger, stronger army he had not planned for will be crushed. Jesus' message is clear: Do not start what you cannot finish! Take a moment and consider your resources before starting a project that may end in humiliating shame or bitter defeat. To use a well-known Pauline image, a disciple must be willing to run the race to the end, and not stop before reaching the finish line.

The third and climactic conditional sentence requires that one renounce, literally, "say farewell to" (see 9:61) possessions. For Luke's community the more difficult cost of discipleship may not have been martyrdom—as might be expected—but the renunciation of all that a person has. In light of vv. 26–27, the term for possessions, *hyparchonta* (v. 33), may include not just a field or oxen (14:18–19), but all that a person has, including family, even one's very life.

The parabolic saying on salt illustrates the fate of the disciple who lacks total commitment to God's prophet. When salt "loses its taste" (literally, "becomes foolish"), it is fit for nothing—neither soil nor manure—except to be thrown out.

The mention of soil recalls the parable of the sower and the seed. Both these parables end in the same way: "Whoever has ears to hear ought to hear" (8:8; 14:35).

For reflection: Monastic traditions from both East and West emphasize a simplicity of life. The cells for monks are not to be cluttered with many possessions for these can distract from pursuit of the Holy. The way that most believers live at the dawn of the twenty-first century is far different from this. As convenient and helpful as contemporary cultural items may be, they also exact a price. Accumulated e-mails demand time to sort through, electronic devices need to be repaired, and cars, boats, and RVs require upkeep. All of these things and many more certainly have their benefits, and in fact, may even seem to be indispensable. Yet, how much do they complicate our lives?

The stark sayings on discipleship offer an important lens through which we can view our relationship to the many things that surround our life and demand attention. Besides material things, there are the multiple human interactions that define a person's daily routine. Whoever becomes so enmeshed with worldly pursuits can become lost on the journey, unwilling to carry the cross and unaware of those who need our service the most, the poor and the marginalized.

The mettle of our discipleship may be measured by keeping in balance two ways—the way of contemplation and the way of action. Is there a place in the rush of our daily life for prayer and contemplation? Do I make the choice to spend time quietly aware of the presence of the living God? As to the way of action, do I spend some of my day engaged in bringing about God's kingdom either through word, deed, or presence?

Parable of the Lost Sons and the Merciful Father (15:1–2, 11–32)

^{15:1} The tax collectors and sinners were all drawing near to listen to him, ² but the Pharisees and scribes began to complain, saying, "This man welcomes sinners and eats with them."

¹¹ Then he said, "A man had two sons, ¹² and the younger son said to his father, 'Father, give me the share of your estate that should come to me.' So the father divided the property between them. ¹³ After a few days, the younger son collected all his belongings and set off to a distant country where he squandered his inheritance on a life of dissipation. ¹⁴ When he had freely spent everything, a severe famine struck that country, and he found himself in dire need. ¹⁵ So he hired himself out to one of the local citizens who sent him to his farm to tend the swine. ¹⁶ And he longed to eat his fill of the pods on which the swine fed, but nobody gave him any. ¹⁷ Coming to his senses he thought, 'How many of my father's hired workers have more than enough food to eat, but here am I, dying from hunger. ¹⁸ I shall get up and go to my father and I shall say to him, "Father, I have sinned against heaven and against you. ¹⁹ I no longer deserve to be called your son; treat me as you would treat one of your hired workers."' ²⁰ So he got up and went back to his father. While he was still a long way off, his father caught sight of him, and was filled with compassion. He ran to his son, embraced him and kissed him. ²¹ His son said to him, 'Father, I have sinned against heaven and against you; I no longer deserve to be called your son.' ²² But his father ordered his servants, 'Quickly bring the finest robe and put it on him; put a ring on his finger and sandals on his feet. ²³ Take the fattened calf and slaughter it. Then let us celebrate with a feast, ²⁴ because this son of mine was dead, and has come to life again; he was lost, and has been found.' Then the celebration began. ²⁵ Now the older son had been out in the field and, on his way back, as he neared the house, he heard the sound of music and dancing. ²⁶ He called one of the servants and asked what this might

mean. [27] The servant said to him, 'Your brother has returned and your father has slaughtered the fattened calf because he has him back safe and sound.' [28] He became angry, and when he refused to enter the house, his father came out and pleaded with him. [29] He said to his father in reply, 'Look, all these years I served you and not once did I disobey your orders; yet you never gave me even a young goat to feast on with my friends. [30] But when your son returns who swallowed up your property with prostitutes, for him you slaughter the fattened calf.' [31] He said to him, 'My son, you are here with me always; everything I have is yours. [32] But now we must celebrate and rejoice, because your brother was dead and has come to life again; he was lost and has been found.' "

One of Luke's most compelling parables is that of the Father and Two Sons. The first two verses of this chapter set the theme. Jesus is surrounded by tax collectors and sinners who have drawn near to listen to him. But this is too much for the Pharisees and scribes to bear, so they accuse Jesus of welcoming sinners and eating with them. If this were a formal trial, Jesus would reply "Guilty as charged."

Jesus defends himself by telling three parables: the lost sheep (15:3–7), the lost coin (15:8–10), and the lost sons (15:11–32). Each one is about seeking out the lost and the offer of God's gracious forgiveness. In none of these is a confession of guilt demanded, breast beating required, or even a penance to be performed. Although the younger son does acknowledge his sinfulness to his father, he is not required to recount his misdeeds. The theme that does resound throughout this chapter is one of joyful celebration. The shepherd rejoices with his friends and neighbors when the lost sheep is found (15:6). So too the woman who lost a coin rejoices with her community (15:9). And finally, the jubilant father calls his reunited sons to celebrate for the lost one has been found (15:32). Rejoicing on earth resounds in heaven where there will be joy among the angels of God (15:7,10).

The opening line of this parable, "A man had two sons," evokes the two-brother stories from the Jewish scriptures in which the younger is victorious over the older one(s). The Jacob and Esau narrative (Gn 25:27–34; 27:1–45) as well as the story of Joseph and his brothers come to mind (Gn 37:1–4). In this vein the older brother in Jesus' parable thinks that his younger brother triumphs over him. The father, however, is deeply and equally concerned for both his sons. Although each has disappointed him greatly, they are still his children, and he strives hard to bring the family together to celebrate the reunion. From the father's perspective the younger son is welcomed back, not to outrank his older sibling, but to rejoin him as brother.

The younger son's request for his share of the inheritance is a sign that all is not well. To request one's inheritance before the time of death is not customary (Sir 33:24); to squander it on self-indulgent behavior is disgraceful. Such action dishonors the father and the son, who, having spent his father's money freely among the Gentiles, no longer has the resources to care for him in old age. The son further disgraced himself by following Gentile ways when he took a job attending to the pigs (see 8:26–39). Dying from hunger, he longed to sustain himself by eating pigs' food, the bitter tasting pods of the carob tree. But even this was denied him.

Having left his family, abandoned his religious heritage, lost his integrity, and now with his life itself threatened, he came to his senses (literally, "to himself"). He decided to return home, hoping to be accepted back not as son, but as servant. Like many who come to the point where they want to reconnect with injured family members, he practiced his soliloquy—hoping to find the right words to achieve his goal. The rest depended on his father.

While he was still a long way off, his waiting father was the first to see him. The father's unwavering expectation reflects how much hope he still had for his son's return. When he finally came into view, the father was filled with compassion. He runs to meet, embraces, and kisses his son. The three action verbs

147

add drama and underscore the father's undying affection. Without reprimand, indignation, or anger, the father receives him back as a son. Before this wayfaring youth can even finish his prepared speech, the father interrupts him and proceeds to honor him with gifts and plans a grand celebration.

The "finest robe" (literally "first robe") may have been the father's best one. The gift of a ring signifies restored trust, and the sandals indicate that he was being received as a free person, not as a slave. This was to be no small celebration. A fatted calf could feed more than a hundred people—the whole village was to join in. If the son, and to some extent the father, felt humiliated in eyes of the villagers at the son's disgraceful behavior, the celebration would go a long way to restore honor to the one who had come back to life again.

After hearing this part of the story the tax collectors and sinners (15:1) must have been greatly reassured. Surely they would have identified with the younger son, and rejoiced in knowing that they would be received enthusiastically by the compassionate father. Contrary to the complaints of the Pharisees and scribes, they are to be warmly welcomed to the royal banquet.

As the celebration gets under way with festive music and dancing, the elder son wonders what is happening. He was returning from the field where he had been dutifully working. After he questioned a servant to get the story, he expressed anger toward his father in every gesture. He refused to enter the house, choosing to stand outside, placing himself in the same situation as those whose behavior kept them locked outside the heavenly banquet (13:25–29). Further, the elder son did not address his father with a title of respect; rather he sarcastically referred to himself as a slave (the literal meaning of "I served you"); and he accused his father of favoritism. His reckless brother was given a calf, but, he charged, his father never so much as gave him a goat for a smaller party with his friends. Then he maligns his brother by saying that he used his inheritance on prostitutes—this was not mentioned in the first part of the story. He also denies having any relationship with him, referring to him as the father's son, and not his brother.

All of this convinces us that the older brother has himself been lost, and out of relationship with his father for some time. Discontent festered in his soul; self-righteousness inhabited his heart. Though insulted and rebuffed, the father responds in terms of endearment, calling him "my son," assuring him of his constant presence, and reminding him that all he has is his. The pledge to share all his possessions with his disgruntled son is the father's way of healing a ruptured relationship. The father is determined to hold together the family, and goes to great lengths to make that happen.

The Pharisees and scribes undoubtedly recognized that the second part of this parable was intended for them. Like the elder son, they remained obedient to the commandments and claimed to have stayed faithful to the covenant. However, out of resentment and discontent they refused to accept Jesus and the message he embodied. They were closed to the good news he brought.

The parable ends on an open-ended note. How will the elder brother, how will the Pharisees and scribes, and how will those in Luke's community who identify with the dutiful son respond to the loving compassion of the father?

For reflection: Through art, story, and countless conversion experiences of reconciliation the parable of the compassionate father with two sons has had a profound impact. This parable works when the reader becomes vulnerable enough to identify with the character with whom he or she feels most uncomfortable.

Each of us is on a different place in the spiritual journey. If we have been wronged in some way by another and are still holding on to the injury with undiminished determination, it may be the merciful father who breaks into our heart and inclines us toward forgiveness and compassion. If we have wandered away from our family, our faith community, even from our real self, the change of heart by the younger son may inspire us to come back to our true home, and there to seek reconciliation with our God and one another. If we, like the older son, have labored faithfully in the vineyard of our vocation, doing our duty day by day, it may be helpful to look into the garden of our soul to see if any seeds of self-righteousness have taken root. Naming our resentments may be a way to get at this.

Through this parable the grace of God's divinely appointed proclaimer is there for all to receive. This parable reminds us that when dead we can be brought back to life again, and when lost, found.

Parable of the Dishonest Steward (Lk 16:1–13)

16:1 Then he also said to his disciples, "A rich man had a steward who was reported to him for squandering his property. 2 He summoned him and said, 'What is this I hear about you? Prepare a full account of your stewardship, because you can no longer be my steward.' 3 The steward said to himself, 'What shall I do, now that my master is taking the position of steward away from me? I am not strong enough to dig and I am ashamed to beg. 4 I know what I shall do so that, when I am removed from the stewardship, they may welcome me into their homes.' 5 He called in his master's debtors one by one. To the first he said, 'How much do you owe my master?' 6 He replied, 'One hundred measures of olive oil.' He said to him, 'Here is your promissory note. Sit down and quickly write one for fifty.' 7 Then to another he said, 'And you, how much do you owe?' He replied, 'One hundred kors of wheat.' He said to him, 'Here is your promissory note; write one for eighty.' 8 And the master commended that dishonest steward for acting prudently.

"For the children of this world are more prudent in dealing with their own generation than are the children of light. 9 I tell you, make friends for yourselves with dishonest wealth, so that when it fails, you will be welcomed into eternal dwellings. 10 The person who is trustworthy in very small matters is also trustworthy in great ones; and the person who is dishonest in very small matters is also dishonest in great ones. [11]If, therefore, you are not trustworthy with dishonest wealth, who will trust you with true wealth? [12]If you are not trustworthy with what belongs to another, who will give you what is yours? [13]No servant can serve two masters. He will either hate one and love the other, or be devoted to one and despise the other. You cannot serve God and mammon."

The unifying theme of chapter 16 is the proper use of possessions. Addressed to the disciples, the two parables begin in the same way: "There was a rich man . . . " (16:1, 19). The Pharisees, called lovers of money, are also within hearing range (16:14). Since it was normally assumed in the first century that a rich person was unjust—having become wealthy through oppression and evildoing—it is ironical that the rich master in the first parable charges his steward with being unjust himself, having squandered his property (16:1). We are not told whether this charge was true. Rather than defending himself, the dismissed steward strategizes about how to save his skin when he becomes homeless and needs hospitality. His soliloquy engages the reader who can only admire him for choosing to act decisively (16:3–4).

Operating on the principle of reciprocity, the steward hopes that his master's debtors will respond favorably to him in exchange for having their debts significantly reduced. These were no small debts. The oil amounted to about nine hundred gallons, and the wheat to over a thousand bushels. Who is taking the loss represented by the reduced promissory notes? The discounted amount is not the commission the steward might have received—note that the debtors are the master's not the steward's. Rather, the reductions probably represent a cancellation of the interest that the steward included in the sale for the purpose of increasing his master's profits. Although the Greco-Roman legal system permitted it, the practice of usury was clearly banned in the Old Testament (Ex 22:24; Lv 25:35–37; Dt 23:20–21).

Surely the debtors would be greatly pleased with the steward's largess. There is every reason to believe that they would reciprocate and generously return the favor to the steward when he was in need.

Rather than beating or chastising his manager, the master praises him—catching contemporary readers by surprise—even though his steward's generosity has just cost him a significant amount of lost revenue! So why then, does the master praise his manager? He does so not because his steward was dishonest, but rather because he acted shrewdly, and in doing so brought increased honor to the master from those who had their debts reduced. What the master lost in profits he gained in honor! The reference to "dishonest" steward in 16:8 does not refer back to the charge made against him at the beginning of the parable (16:1), but to his unauthorized action in marking down the debts.

To this parable Luke has added three sayings from Jesus about the prudent use of wealth (16:8b–9), the importance of fidelity (16:10–12), and the incompatibility of serving God while being a slave to riches (16:13). Well-off Christians in Luke's community are instructed to make friends with the poor by using their "dishonest wealth" (literally: "mammon of iniquity") to give alms to the needy. In this way they will be converting their unjust gain into heavenly capital. And the poor, who will be at Abraham's side in the kingdom (see 16:23), will welcome them into the eternal dwellings (literally: "eternal tents"). The concluding statement about not being able to serve both God and mammon underscores the conviction that each is an absolute master claiming exclusive loyalty. To love one means rejecting the other.

For reflection: Through this parable Jesus praises those who, like the steward, act resourcefully during times of crisis. The disciples of Jesus are to act decisively by using their material resources on behalf of the poor. In his own need the steward reached out to others. He realized that his wealth was not in his master's accounts, but rather in establishing relationships within the community. Rather than being "lovers of money," believers are challenged to discern how to put material resources at the service of others. Those who regularly and faithfully do this demonstrate that they serve God; those who choose not to do so become enslaved by what they have. The ways that individuals, families, or households respond to the call to share will differ. In what concrete way are you being called to be generous?

The Parable of the Rich Man and Lazarus (Lk 16:19–31)

[19] "There was a rich man who dressed in purple garments and fine linen and dined sumptuously each day. [20] And lying at his door was a poor man named Lazarus, covered with sores, [21] who would gladly have eaten his fill of the scraps that fell from the rich man's table. Dogs even used to come and lick his sores. [22] When the poor man died, he was carried away by angels to the bosom of Abraham. The rich man also died and was buried, [23] and from the netherworld, where he was in torment, he raised his eyes and saw Abraham far off and Lazarus at his side. [24] And he cried out, 'Father Abraham, have pity on me. Send Lazarus to dip the tip of his finger in water and cool my tongue, for I am suffering torment in these flames.' [25] Abraham replied, 'My child, remember that you received what was good during your lifetime while Lazarus likewise received what was bad; but now he is comforted here, whereas you are tormented. [26] Moreover, between us and you a great chasm is established to prevent anyone from crossing who might wish to go from our side to yours or from your side to ours.' [27] He said, 'Then I beg you, father, send him to my father's house, [28] for I have five brothers, so that he may warn them, lest they too come to this place of torment.' [29] But Abraham replied, 'They have Moses and the prophets. Let them listen to them.' [30] He said, 'Oh no, father Abraham, but if someone from the dead goes to them, they will repent.' [31] Then Abraham said, 'If they will not listen to Moses and

the prophets, neither will they be persuaded if someone should rise from the dead.' "

The second parable in chapter 16 poignantly addresses the lasting consequences of the rich who fail to respond to the poor in their midst. Luke draws a sharp contrast between two people on opposite ends of the socio-economic ladder. The rich man, also known in popular tradition as Dives (from the Latin Vulgate for rich man), was luxuriously clothed; he feasted sumptuously every day. On the other hand there was poor Lazarus, a name that means "God has helped," who lay sick with a body full of sores, hungry, and unclean from the dogs who licked his sores. While the rich man had five brothers, Lazarus evidently had no family of his own.

This story is a compelling illustration of the reversal of fortunes proclaimed in the beatitudes and woes (6:20–21, 24–25). Lazarus' desire to be satisfied (16:21) is identical to what the hungry are promised (6:21): the passive form of the verb *chortazō* ("to be satisfied") is used in both verses. After death Lazarus, who once lay unnoticed and neglected at the rich man's table, has a place of comfort in the kingdom. On the other hand, the rich man who regularly feasted at his banquet table now experiences eternal torment in the netherworld.

Ironically, although the rich man never noticed Lazarus lying at his own door, in the afterlife he sees Lazarus far off at Abraham's side (literally, "at his bosom"). Lying at one's bosom or chest suggests comfort, care and intimacy. It is a desired position at the heavenly banquet (see 13:28–29; Jn 13:22). Three times the rich man begs Father Abraham to send Lazarus for help: first for a bit of water, then to warn his brothers, and finally to plea again that his brothers might repent (16:24, 27, 30). The first appeal also contains a poignant irony. The rich man pleads for mercy from the heavenly patriarch even though he had no mercy for Lazarus in his need.

In the three responses Abraham offers wise counsel to those who would listen. First he affirms the reversal of fortunes and underscores the unbridgeable chasm between the realms of triumph and torment. Secondly, he asserts that Moses and the prophets are warning enough about the urgent call to serve the poor (see e.g., Dt 15:1–11; Is 58:6–7). And finally, Abraham insists that those who ignore the scriptures will hardly pay attention to one who has risen from the dead. For Luke this last declaration is a clear reference to Jesus whom God has raised up.

For reflection: Sometimes it is said that the Lukan Jesus offers a blanket condemnation to all the rich. This is not case. The rich man in this parable is punished not because he happens to be wealthy but because he refused to see Lazarus at his very door step. He had the means to alleviate his hunger and to comfort him in his suffering but he did not. The parable addresses the five brothers and all those who are still on their pilgrimage through life. There is still an opportunity to repent, and this means to show concern for the poor. To ignore the poor puts one's life in peril. It is helpful to become aware of one's own discomfort when this parable is heard. For the feeling of such dis-ease may well be the beginning of a positive response to those who are proclaimed blessed in the kingdom of God.

Attitude of a Servant (17:5–10)

⁵ And the apostles said to the Lord, "Increase our faith." ⁶ The Lord replied, "If you have faith the size of a mustard seed, you would say to [this] mulberry tree, 'Be uprooted and planted in the sea,' and it would obey you.
⁷ "Who among you would say to your servant who has just come in from plowing or tending sheep in the field, 'Come here immediately and take your place at table'? ⁸ Would he not rather say to him, 'Prepare something for me to eat. Put on your apron and wait on me while I eat and drink. You may eat and drink when I am finished'? ⁹ Is he grateful to that servant because he did what was commanded? ¹⁰ So should it be with you. When you have done all you have been

commanded, say, 'We are unprofitable servants; we have done what we were obliged to do.' "

This section ends on a theme similar to the way it began in 13:22–30: being a disciple requires vigilance, commitment, and loyalty. Jesus warns the disciples sternly about the dire consequences of leading another disciple, "one of these little ones," astray (17:1–2). In a hyperbolic statement, Jesus asserts that death by drowning is preferable to causing another to sin, meaning here to give up one's faith (17:2). Then, taking a less harsh, more pastoral stance, Jesus offers guidance on how to heal relationships (17:3–4). When a believer does sin, the disciple is to offer correction; then, if the person repents, to extend forgiveness. Forgiveness is not a one time event, but is to be offered seven times a day, or without limit (see Mt 18:22).

Hearing this, the apostles are wondering whether they have the kind of faith that such a way of life demands. Faith in this section can be understood as undivided loyalty to the Master. Jesus teaches that there is no need to have more faith, only to use the little bit of faith one already has (17:6). Even a small mustard-seed amount of faith can do marvelous things, comparable to uprooting and planting a mulberry tree, a large tree known to have an extended root system.

In a parable about a slave and his master (17:7–10), Jesus first asks the apostles to put themselves in the place of the owner and consider what was to be expected. Maybe some members of Luke's own community were slave owners. Recall that in the first century slaves would normally not dine with their master. Rather, in a single-slave household, a slave who finishes the plowing or tending the sheep was then expected to do the cooking when he returned from the field. Identifying with the masters, the apostles, who represent the leaders of Luke's church, would readily agree.

This, however, sets them up for a surprising shift at the parable's end. Now, the apostles are asked to identify with the slave. To be leader is to be servant. As slaves in the kingdom they themselves should not expect to be served, thanked or praised. Rather, they are to say that we are servants "without need" (the literal translation of the Greek, rendered here by the NAB as "unprofitable"). Neither the apostles nor the church leaders of Luke's day are to receive any special privilege, favor or honor for doing what is expected of them. Earlier, Jesus spoke about the unusual situation of a master waiting on the slave (12:35–37). But now he is further on his journey toward Jerusalem where he will meet suffering and death. Loyalty and commitment are required; privilege at the table is not to be claimed. Like Jesus, the disciple is called to be among others "as the one who serves" (22:27).

For reflection: It is only human to expect—even for church leaders who conscientiously lead the faithful—to be rewarded for one's labors or at least to be appreciated. In a culture that fosters a mentality of entitlement or privilege for those in positions of authority, the challenge of Jesus to the apostles is to surrender all such aspirations. While this challenge may apply especially to church leaders, it also extends to all those who have been sent as ambassadors for the kingdom.

This parable provides rich images for the work of prophets, disciples and apostles. Plowing the field, tending sheep, and serving meals symbolically illustrate the work of the kingdom. Luke readily uses these: plowing (9:62), shepherding the flock (Acts 20:28), and being slaves of God (Acts 4:29; 16:17). What image, one of these or another, best portrays your role as a herald of the kingdom?

VI

The End of the Travel Narrative and Jesus' Teaching in Jerusalem
(17:11– 21:38)

Jesus continues on his way toward Jerusalem traveling through towns and villages bringing the good news. During the final segment of his journey he heals ten lepers (17:11–19), requires vigilance for the sudden coming of the Son of Man (17:22–37), offers two parables on prayer (18:1–14), and a parable about inheriting eternal life (18:18–30). The third passion prediction makes the announced Jerusalem events seem very near and disturbing (18:31–34). Then on the road to Jericho the blind beggar was healed, able to see because of his faith (18:35–43). The encounter with Zacchaeus reminds us that Jesus' mission was to seek out the lost (19:1–10).

Jesus tells the parable of the ten gold coins to instill in those who would hear that acceptance or rejection of him will bring life or death (19:11–27). Then finally arriving at the outskirts of Jerusalem, Jesus instructs two disciples to prepare for his entry into the city where the very stones will cry out (19:28–40). In two very different responses, Jesus weeps over the city that will find no peace (19:41–44) and then lays claim to the temple by driving out the den of thieves (19:45–48).

Jesus defends his authority (20:1–8) and continues teaching through parable and discourse about loyalty to God and the resurrection (20:9–44). Chastising the scribes for defrauding widows (20:45–47), he praises a poor widow for her generosity and detachment (21:1–4). This section concludes with an extended teaching about signs leading up to end-time events (21:5–38).

The Cleansing of Ten Lepers (17:11–19)

[11] As he continued his journey to Jerusalem, he traveled through Samaria and Galilee. [12] As he was entering a village, ten lepers met [him]. They stood at a distance from him [13] and raised their voice, saying, "Jesus, Master! Have pity on us!" [14] And when he saw them, he said, "Go show yourselves to the priests." As they were going they were cleansed. [15] And one of them, realizing he had been healed, returned, glorifying God in a loud voice; [16] and he fell at the feet of Jesus and thanked him. He was a Samaritan. [17] Jesus said in reply, "Ten were cleansed, were they not? Where are the other nine? [18] Has none but this foreigner returned to give thanks to God?" [19] Then he said to him, "Stand up and go; your faith has saved you."

While Jesus was traveling across the borderland between Galilee and Samaria, ten lepers approached him. Given the geographical location, it is not surprising that one of them was a Samaritan, although we are not told this until the latter part of the story. Because of the social and religious boundaries imposed between lepers and the rest of the community (see Lv 13:45–46), it is understandable that they would keep themselves at a distance from Jesus. Still, they do not hesitate to make their request known.

Addressing Jesus as Master with raised voices they plead: "Have pity on us!" In the Mediterranean world to ask for mercy from another is to tap into that person's capacity to meet expected interpersonal obligations. What they are seeking from Jesus is his ability to restore them to full membership in the community. They recognize that Jesus, as God's agent of healing, is able to do that. Jesus promptly responds by instructing them to go show themselves to the priests who were the gatekeepers of the purity laws established to protect human boundaries of bodily contact (see Lv 14:1–32). This must have taken some faith on the part of the lepers because they are not cured until after they start on their way to the priests.

159

While all ten were aware of their cure, only one realized the full extent of what happened. Beyond the physical cure, he was healed, that is restored to wholeness—for he had received God's salvation. A fitting response to being either cured or healed would be to offer sacrifice in the Temple. Instead this person returns to Jesus and glorified God in a loud voice, praising God for what God's prophet accomplished in him. Praise of God is the characteristic response in Luke of those who have experienced divine power and mercy (2:20; 5:25, 26; 7:16; 13:13; 18:43; 23:47; Acts 4:21; 21:20).

The Samaritan expressed praise by his bodily posture, falling at the feet of Jesus. His praise blossomed into heartfelt thanksgiving. To say thank you is to confirm and to extend the relationship that has been formed. We are naturally drawn to admire this grateful person who glorified God by thanking Jesus. But then the unexpected is disclosed. We learn that he was a Samaritan, an outsider excluded from the community because of his ethnicity (see 9:51–56; 10:33; Acts 8:4–25). As a Samaritan this foreigner would not be welcome to worship in the Temple. Yet Jesus praises him, and in doing so challenges whatever negative stereotypes the believing community may have harbored toward outsiders.

Jesus announces this person's salvation: "Your faith has saved you." Closely linking one's faith response with the salvation received, this affirmation is also applied by Luke to two women and two men in his Gospel (7:50; 8:48; 17:19; 18:42). Faith in Jesus brought this Samaritan cure for his disease, healing from his isolation, and restoration to the community of faith. In encountering Jesus he experienced in a powerful way God's goodness and healing.

For reflection: Once again Jesus identifies as an example of faith a person from outside the chosen community. Thus, this Samaritan becomes a model in his attitude of praise and gratitude to God. Like the story of the Good Samaritan, this story challenges disciples who tend to establish rigid boundaries between insiders and outsiders. As a believing community we are continually called to conversion by reflecting on those whom we have excluded from our midst. Maybe these are the very ones whom God has put there to remind us of the expansive reach of divine mercy and favor. Who lies outside the boundaries of our faith-based community? If we look again, are we able to see how the God of Jesus Christ may well have restored them to wholeness? Our God is one who longs, through our welcome, to include them in the community of faith.

The Day of the Son of Man (17:20–37)

[20] Asked by the Pharisees when the kingdom of God would come, he said in reply, "The coming of the kingdom of God cannot be observed, [21] and no one will announce, 'Look, here it is,' or, 'There it is.' For behold, the kingdom of God is among you."

[22] Then he said to his disciples, "The days will come when you will long to see one of the days of the Son of Man, but you will not see it. [23] There will be those who will say to you, 'Look, there he is,' [or] 'Look, here he is.' Do not go off, do not run in pursuit. [24] For just as lightning flashes and lights up the sky from one side to the other, so will the Son of Man be [in his day]. [25] But first he must suffer greatly and be rejected by this generation. [26] As it was in the days of Noah, so it will be in the days of the Son of Man; [27] they were eating and drinking, marrying and giving in marriage up to the day that Noah entered the ark, and the flood came and destroyed them all. [28] Similarly, as it was in the days of Lot: they were eating, drinking, buying, selling, planting, building; [29] on the day when Lot left Sodom, fire and brimstone rained from the sky to destroy them all. [30] So it will be on the day the Son of Man is revealed. [31] On that day, a person who is on the housetop and whose belongings are in the house must not go down to get them, and likewise a person in the field must not return to what was left behind. [32] Remember the wife of Lot.

³³ Whoever seeks to preserve his life will lose it, but whoever loses it will save it. ³⁴I tell you, on that night there will be two people in one bed; one will be taken, the other left. ³⁵ And there will be two women grinding meal together; one will be taken, the other left." ^{[36] 37}They said to him in reply, "Where, Lord?" He said to them, "Where the body is, there also the vultures will gather."

This is the second of three passages about the coming of the Son of Man and the end of time (12:35–13:9; 21:5–36). The emphasis here is on the suddenness of his coming (17:22–25) and the unhappy fate of those who are not prepared (17:26–37). The topic is unwittingly introduced by Jesus' opponents who inquire when the kingdom will come. Contrary to their pattern of meticulously investigating God's prophet, Jesus warns them that the coming of divine rule is not to be discerned by close observation. Faith in Jesus, not skeptical scrutiny, is required. There will be no marquee announcing that the kingdom is either here or there. Indeed, the kingdom is already "among" you. The Greek can also be translated "within" you. For those with eyes to see and ears to hear it is already present in Jesus' healing and preaching ministry.

Yet there is a difference between God's rule as manifested by Jesus and its full realization at the end. In the rest of this passage Jesus turns his attention to the disciples and instructs them about the future coming of the kingdom. Although they may not see the Son of Man arrive when they long for it, that day will come nonetheless. That day will be as sudden and brilliant as lightning flashes across the sky. No one will miss it! However, this will not occur immediately, for first the Son of Man must suffer greatly and be rejected.

Not only will the Son of Man be despised in Jerusalem, he will also be rejected by those whose lives are consumed with business as usual such as eating, drinking, and marrying. These daily activities, though not judged as negative in themselves, are not to distract from an active anticipation of Jesus' return.

Like in the days of Noah and the flood, believers need to be vigilant lest they end up losing their lives. The reference to Lot includes four activities related to possessions: buying, selling, planting, and building (17:28), recalling the parables of the rich farmer and the great feast (12:16–21; 14:15–24). When the Son of Man comes those whose lives are absorbed by possessions will be like those in Lot's day who were consumed by fire and brimstone. Neither those on the housetop nor in the field are to be trapped by what is left behind. They are not to be like Lot's wife who identified her life with her possessions. Jesus reiterates a paradox at the heart of the Gospel: those who seek to preserve life will lose it, whereas those who lose it will preserve life (literally: "keep it alive"; see 9:24–25). The last saying about the body and a vulture underscores the certainty of the Son of Man's coming. Just as the sight of a vulture in the sky is a sure sign of a corpse on the ground, so also the kingdom of God can be found wherever the faithful are gathered in vigilance awaiting the Son of Man.

For reflection: This Gospel passage is probably not the favorite among believers—except for those who preach a message of fire and brimstone. Still, it has its place. Every baptized believer is called by God to be vigilant. Whether young or old no one can say with certainty when death will come. Who among us is assured of living to the end of this day? Constant vigilance implies the need for ongoing conversion. This passage calls us to re-evaluate our priorities in light of the Gospel. How am I called to turn more fully to Gospel values? What habits or possessions do I need to let go of so that I can be ready to welcome the Son of Man?

Two Parables on Prayer (18:1–14)

18:1 Then he told them a parable about the necessity for them to pray always without becoming weary. He said, 2 "There was a judge in a certain town who neither feared God nor respected any human being. [3] And a widow in that town used to come to him and say, 'Render a just decision for me against my adversary.' [4] For a long time the judge was unwilling, but eventually he thought, 'While it is true that I neither fear God nor respect any human being, [5] because this widow keeps bothering me I shall deliver a just decision for her lest she finally come and strike me.' " [6] The Lord said, "Pay attention to what the dishonest judge says. [7] Will not God then secure the rights of his chosen ones who call out to him day and night? Will he be slow to answer them? [8] I tell you, he will see to it that justice is done for them speedily. But when the Son of Man comes, will he find faith on earth?"

[9] He then addressed this parable to those who were convinced of their own righteousness and despised everyone else. [10] "Two people went up to the temple area to pray; one was a Pharisee and the other was a tax collector. [11] The Pharisee took up his position and spoke this prayer to himself, 'O God, I thank you that I am not like the rest of humanity— greedy, dishonest, adulterous—or even like this tax collector. [12] I fast twice a week, and I pay tithes on my whole income.' [13] But the tax collector stood off at a distance and would not even raise his eyes to heaven but beat his breast and prayed, 'O God, be merciful to me a sinner.' [14] I tell you, the latter went home justified, not the former; for everyone who exalts himself will be humbled, and the one who humbles himself will be exalted."

Luke's Gospel contains a rich treasure of prayers (1:46–55, 68–79; 2:14, 29–32; 11:2–4) and teachings on prayer (11:5–13). These two parables instruct us about persistence (18:1–8) and the right attitude to have when petitioning God (18:9–14). In the first parable a widow is pitted against a powerful judge, in the second a Pharisee, expected to be a paragon of piety, is contrasted to a tax collector, one expected to know little about prayer.

Jesus begins by stating the point of the first parable: the necessity to pray always and not to become weary (literally, "not to lose heart"). If anyone had reason to despair, it would be the widow whose case was before a judge who neither feared God nor respected others. Widows were without the protection or financial support of a husband; hence they were likely to be poor and vulnerable to exploitation (see 7:11–17; 20:47; 21:1–4). Their socio-economic status was precarious and their needs often neglected. For this reason the Torah instructs that the cry of the widow be heard and her rights respected (Ex 22:21–23; Dt 24:17). Those who oppressed them are subject to divine wrath (Ps 94:1–7; Jb 22:9–11; Is 1:16–17, 21–25). However, since the judge in this passage did not fear God, the widow could hardly hope to obtain a sympathetic hearing for her case.

In Luke widows are not stereotyped as powerless; rather they are noted for their piety (2:36–38), for their detachment from material possessions (21:1–4), and in this case, as models for persistence in prayer. The early church seems to have established an order of widows giving them a status that they may not have had otherwise in society (Acts 6:1; 9:36–43). Evidently without an advocate of her own, this widow in the parable kept bothering the judge so that he finally decided to deliver a just decision. The added motivation, "lest she finally come and strike me," is quite unexpected, and almost comical. Literally this means "to strike under the eye," or "to give a black eye" as a boxer or bully would. In his soliloquy the judge got the picture. This widow, willing to go to extreme lengths, was not to be denied.

Reasoning from the lesser to the greater, Jesus argues that if an unjust judge yields to the persistent quest of a widow whose case seemed hopeless, how much more will a caring and gracious God respond favorably to the prayer of the disciples. The last verse suggests that faith in Luke's community was faltering because of the delayed return of the Son of Man. Not to be discouraged, they are to remain faithful for they will see justice done by God.

The second parable (18:9–14) is addressed to those who are convinced of their superiority, while despising all others. A sharp contrast is drawn between two individuals, a Pharisee and tax collector. At first glance the Pharisee's actions appear to be commendable: he is thankful, he observes the command-ments—not being greedy, dishonest, or adulterous—he fasts, and he pays tithes. In many ways he is a model parishioner, especially for a pastor who is concerned about the support of the church. From all appearances the Pharisee's behavior can hardly be faulted.

Yet, his motivation for thankfulness exposes his heart. Considering himself to be better than the rest of humanity, he harbors a critical attitude that regards others with contempt. Through self praise he displays his self-righteousness. Since he judges himself to be righteous, he has no need of God's mercy.

The tax collector, on the other hand, demonstrates by his position "at a distance," and by his action of beating his breast (see also 23:48), that he is repentant and in need of God's reconciling grace. The Pharisee's prayer is long, recounting good deeds whereas the tax collector's prayer is short, acknowl-edging his sinfulness. Surprisingly, Jesus declares that the tax collector is acquitted in God's court of justice and thus declared righteous, and not the Pharisee. This recalls the contrast between Simon the Pharisee and the sinful woman (7:36–50).

Jesus uses this parable to defend his ministry to sinners, represented by the tax collector and to warn those who like this Pharisee justify themselves. The story is not meant just for Jesus' opponents but addresses his disciples as well. Luke would have in mind all those in his community who place their trust in themselves rather than in God who offers his free gift of grace.

For reflection: In difficult times we may readily turn to prayer at first, but if circumstances do not change quickly for the better, there is a temptation to lose heart and despair. We may even begin to think that God is really like this unjust judge who does not care and is slow to respond. The gutsy determination of this widow is a welcome reminder to be persistent in boldly bringing our case before God. Our prayer is to be neither timid nor sporadic. Like the widow this story reminds us that God does hear the cry of those who call out to the Holy One. For many of us who faithfully follow Jesus on the journey, keeping the commandments and fulfilling our obligations, it is easy to fall into a mentality that compares our virtuous actions favorably to those whose lives seem to be far less religious or even spiritual. Honestly identifying with the Pharisee may be the first step for a deep conversion of heart.

The Rich Official (18:18–30)

[18] An official asked him this question, "Good teacher, what must I do to inherit eternal life?" [19] Jesus answered him, "Why do you call me good? No one is good but God alone. [20] You know the commandments, 'You shall not commit adultery; you shall not kill; you shall not steal; you shall not bear false witness; honor your father and your mother.'" [21] And he replied, "All of these I have observed from my youth." [22] When Jesus heard this he said to him, "There is still one thing left for you: sell all that you have and distribute it to the poor, and you will have a treasure in heaven. Then come, follow me." [23] But when he heard this he became quite sad, for he was very rich.

[24] Jesus looked at him [now sad] and said, "How hard it is for those who have wealth to enter the kingdom of God! [25] For it is easier for a camel to pass through the eye of a needle than for a rich person to enter the kingdom of God." [26] Those who heard this said, "Then who can be saved?" [27] And he said, "What is impossible for human beings is possible for God." [28] Then Peter said, "We have given up our possessions and followed you." [29] He said to them, "Amen, I say to you, there is no one who has given up house or wife or brothers or parents or children for the sake of the kingdom of God [30] who will not receive [back] an overabundant return in this present age and eternal life in the age to come."

The family scene of people bringing infants to Jesus to touch them (18:15–17) sets the stage for this parable. Overriding the disciples' effort to keep the kids away, Jesus gathered the children around him and emphatically announced that the kingdom of God is to be accepted like a child. Because little ones have an attitude of humility they, like the tax collector, will enter the kingdom. In a remarkable contrast to these children, who know nothing of power, status and wealth, stands the official (literally, "ruler") in this story who can lay claim to all three. The other framing passage to this parable is the third passion prediction (18:31–34). Childlike simplicity and the willingness to lose one's life are the necessary qualities to enter the kingdom.

The ruler inquires what he must do to inherit eternal life. Although the text does not specify, he may well have been a religious leader, similar to those Jesus encounters elsewhere (8:41; 14:1; 23:13, 35; 24:20). By upgrading his status to "ruler" and describing him as "very rich" (compare Mk 10:17–31), Luke may well have in mind those high-ranking and wealthy members of his community who were interested in following the Christian way. The ruler calls Jesus "good," but Jesus refuses this honor because God alone is to be worshiped (see 4:8) and is the source of all goodness. Jesus then recites five commandments of the Decalogue, those that govern human relationships. Similar to the Pharisee of the preceding parable, the official claims that his ethical credentials are commendable: he has kept the commandments.

To this Jesus adds a more radical requirement—to sell all that he has. Luke alone among the evangelists intensifies this command by adding "all." Jesus then makes two further demands. The first is to sell what he has and distribute this to the poor. Such giving meets the needs of the destitute and creates solidarity in a community separated by the haves and have nots. Doing this will provide a true and lasting treasure in heaven (see 12:21, 32–33). The second demand is one of discipleship. The renunciation of possessions is an important step in following after Jesus (5:11, 28). Rather than heeding Jesus' call, this man became sad for he could not dispose of his wealth.

The rich ruler stayed around to hear Jesus' reply, the question from the crowd, and Peter's declaration of discipleship. Jesus illustrates the challenge a wealthy person faces in entering the kingdom by comparing this to the difficulty that a camel, Palestine's largest animal, has in entering the smallest of known openings. The crowd, assuming that the rich have an advantage because their possessions were a sure sign of God's benefits, then ask whether anyone can be saved. In response Jesus offers this theological reflection: with God's help it is possible to leave possessions behind. Whoever does this is promised a reward in this life that exceeds the sacrifice and eternal life in the age to come.

For reflection: The rich man attempted to worship God and mammon simultaneously. But when put to the test it became clear that wealth was his real master. He may have kept the second half of the Decalogue but he failed to keep the greatest of the commandments, to love God and neighbor (10:25–28). He was not able to trust God completely nor was he willing to assist his neighbors most in need. Those who identify with this rich ruler may feel sad as he did, not able to follow the requirement of discipleship. However, this passage contains much hope. For with God who is good and wants good things for his children, whether rich or poor, all things are possible.

Zacchaeus the Tax Collector (19:1–10)

19:1 He came to Jericho and intended to pass through the town. ²Now a man there named Zacchaeus, who was a chief tax collector and also a wealthy man, ³was seeking to see who Jesus was; but he could not see him because of the crowd, for he was short in stature. ⁴So he ran ahead and climbed a syca-more tree in order to see Jesus, who was about to pass that way. ⁵When he reached the place, Jesus looked up and said to

him, "Zacchaeus, come down quickly, for today I must stay at your house." [6] And he came down quickly and received him with joy. [7] When they all saw this, they began to grumble, saying, "He has gone to stay at the house of a sinner." [8] But Zacchaeus stood there and said to the Lord, "Behold, half of my possessions, Lord, I shall give to the poor, and if I have extorted anything from anyone I shall repay it four times over." [9] And Jesus said to him, "Today salvation has come to this house because this man too is a descendant of Abraham. [10] For the Son of Man has come to seek and to save what was lost."

Luke moves from the story of the blind beggar (18:35–43) to that of a rich tax collector (19:1–10). Both, in welcoming God's prophet, received salvation—the beggar by his faith, and Zacchaeus by inviting Jesus into his home after pledging to share his possessions. In contrast to the story of the rich ruler (18:18–23), the Zacchaeus episode demonstrates that Jesus makes possible what seems humanly impossible for the rich (18:27): Zacchaeus gets through the needle's eye and experiences salvation. By detaching himself from much of his wealth Zacchaeus demonstrates the necessary disposition of heart. He joyfully received Jesus.

Zacchaeus is described as a chief tax collector, meaning that he probably functioned as a district manager responsible for collecting taxes in a designated region with assistants working under him. Hearing about his position and his wealth, the readers' first reaction to him would probably be negative. However, a fuller picture of Zacchaeus gives rise to a more sympathetic response. He is a short guy who decides to run ahead and climbs a tree so that he can see Jesus. His energetic, enthusiastic response inspires others to overcome obstacles in their quest to encounter God's prophet.

Looking up, Jesus not only notices Zacchaeus but boldly invites himself to stay at his house. Jesus' invitation is not an option, for he says: "I *must* stay at your house." Behind this invitation is the same divine necessity that determines Jesus' own suffering and death. In marked contrast to the sad countenance of the rich ruler, Zacchaeus joyfully accepts Jesus' offer. As has happened before in Luke's story, those who saw this could not tolerate the Master's association with sinners, and so they grumbled (see 5:27–32; 15:1–32). Rising to his own defense, Zacchaeus answers the critics by pledging concrete action as a sign of his conversion.

The present tense of the verbs "I give" and "I repay" (19:8, translated by the NAB as future tense) may imply either that Zacchaeus already does this on a regular basis or that he will do so in the immediate future. The first understanding implies that he does not accept the accusation that he is a sinner. The second interpretation is, however, more probable. The crowd's objection and Jesus' promise of salvation to Zacchaeus that very day suggests that he is a sinner in need of conversion. His decision to distribute half his possessions to the poor and to compensate fourfold those whom he defrauded is held up by Luke as commendable. Having done this Zacchaeus would probably be left with little to call his own.

Jesus confers on him true membership in the people of Israel by calling him a son of Abraham (19:9; see 1:54–55, 68–75). The one who was rejected is now included among the people to whom God's promises have been made. Zacchaeus' desire to find Jesus (19:3) is abundantly granted by Jesus whose own quest is to seek out the lost (19:10).

For reflection: Zacchaeus is a rambunctious, engaging and likable character. How easy it is to imagine this short, rather dignified fellow running through a hostile crowd and climbing a tree to see the one to whom his heart is called. His action dramatizes Augustine's spiritual insight addressed in this prayer to God: "You have made us for yourself, and our heart is restless until it rests in you." What is it that really satisfies the deepest longing of the human heart? Many paths have been tried, some running after greater wealth, increased power, or acclaimed

171

success, some pursuing personal projects that promote one's own well-being, and others striving after a kind of self-justifying perfection.

The Zacchaeus story invites us to reflect on the roads we have taken. What are we running after? Given the pace of life many lead, this running can almost be taken literally. Am I on the path that leads toward wholeness and salvation? If not, what course corrections do I need to take? What might it mean for us to accept Jesus' statement that he "must" dwell in our home?

The Entry into Jerusalem (19:28–48)

Luke sets the stage for Jesus' entry into Jerusalem with a parable about a nobleman who went off to a distant country to become king, and then was rejected when he returned (19:11–27). Like the nobleman, Jesus will be acclaimed as king (19:38; 23:3, 37, 38, 42) and will be despised, because the kingdom of God he embodies will not be understood or welcomed. Jesus is indeed a king, one who brings God's peace (19:28–40), a peace rejected by the people of Jerusalem (19:41–44) and by the merchants in the temple (19:45–48).

 [28]After he had said this, he proceeded on his journey up to Jerusalem. [29]As he drew near to Bethphage and Bethany at the place called the Mount of Olives, he sent two of his disciples. [30]He said, "Go into the village opposite you, and as you enter it you will find a colt tethered on which no one has ever sat. Untie it and bring it here. [31]And if anyone should ask you, 'Why are you untying it?' you will answer, 'The Master has need of it.' " [32]So those who had been sent went off and found everything just as he had told them. [33]And as they were untying the colt, its owners said to them, "Why are you untying this colt?" [34]They answered, "The Master has need of it." [35]So they brought it to Jesus, threw their cloaks over the colt, and helped Jesus to mount. [36]As he rode along, the people were spreading their cloaks on the road; [37] and now as he was

approaching the slope of the Mount of Olives, the whole multitude of his disciples began to praise God aloud with joy for all the mighty deeds they had seen. [38] They proclaimed:
"Blessed is the king who comes in the name of the Lord.
Peace in heaven
and glory in the highest."
[39] Some of the Pharisees in the crowd said to him, "Teacher, rebuke your disciples." [40] He said in reply, "I tell you, if they keep silent, the stones will cry out!"

[41] As he drew near, he saw the city and wept over it, [42] saying, "If this day you only knew what makes for peace—but now it is hidden from your eyes. [43] For the days are coming upon you when your enemies will raise a palisade against you; they will encircle you and hem you in on all sides. [44] They will smash you to the ground and your children within you, and they will not leave one stone upon another within you because you did not recognize the time of your visitation."

[45] Then Jesus entered the temple area and proceeded to drive out those who were selling things, [46] saying to them, "It is written, 'My house shall be a house of prayer, but you have made it a den of thieves.' " [47] And every day he was teaching in the temple area. The chief priests, the scribes, and the leaders of the people, meanwhile, were seeking to put him to death, [48] but they could find no way to accomplish their purpose because all the people were hanging on his words.

Ever since 9:51 Jesus has been on a journey to Jerusalem. Arriving near the villages of Bethphage and Bethany on the eastern side of this city, he gives concrete instructions about how he intended to enter. Although there is no explicit reference to Zechariah 9:9, this text proclaims that Jerusalem's king will come as a savior mounted on a colt. Jesus knows in advance what he instructs two of his disciples to find. When the colt is prepared, Jesus rides along while on the road before him the people spread their cloaks, the most valuable garment they would have owned. This was customarily done when a new king was proclaimed (2 Kgs 9:13).

As Jesus approached the Mount of Olives a large multitude of disciples praised God with joy for the mighty deeds they had witnessed (19:37; see 4:18–19; 7:22). Their king had indeed conquered the enemies of sickness, poverty, and death by curing the blind, the lame, and the crippled, by raising the dead to life, and by bringing the good news to the poor. In response to these mighty deeds the multitude offers praise by citing Psalm 118:26, a verse customarily sung by pilgrims to the holy city. Named to the throne of David and called Son of David earlier in the Gospel (1:32; 18:38, 39), Jesus is now explicitly acclaimed as king—a title added by Luke to the psalm. Then, echoing the angels' joyful announcement of Jesus' birth (2:14), the disciples herald Jesus as one who brings the peace of heaven although this peace is not received on earth, at least not now in Jerusalem (19:41–44).

Some of the Pharisees cannot tolerate this jubilant outcry because proclaiming Jesus as king could cause a popular uprising and this would evoke the wrath of the Romans. But for Jesus now is not the time for silence (see 9:20–21), for if no human voice is raised even the stones will announce his arrival (19:39–40).

From a high vantage point overlooking the city Jesus pours out his sorrow in tears. Full of pathos, Jesus personifies Jerusalem, addressing the city directly: "if *you* only knew . . . hidden from *your* eyes . . . *your* enemies will raise . . . against *you* . . . will encircle *you* . . . *your* children within *you*" (19:42–44). Jesus warns Jerusalem that failure to recognize "your visitation," that is God's prophet, will result in its destruction, probably a reference to the sack of the city and its temple by the Romans in 70 C.E. The multiple parallels between this passage and the Benedictus (compare "visitation" in 1:68, 78 and 19:44; "peace" in 1:79 and 19:42; saved from/encircled by enemies in 1:71, 74 and 19:43; knowledge of salvation and failure to know in 1:77 and 19:42, 44) show that the vision for salvation proclaimed early in the Gospel is being lost, at least for now. And so Jesus weeps over the city.

174

Jesus' destination is the Temple. This sacred place needs to be cleansed of the unrighteous so that Jesus can use it as a place for teaching (20:1–21:38; see 22:53). God's prophet becomes a clear sign of division: the chief priests, the scribes, and the leaders of the people plot to kill Jesus; but they cannot for all the people were hanging on to his every word. By entering the Temple and restoring it to a house of prayer, the temple becomes what it was really meant to be.

For reflection: The ongoing turmoil in Jerusalem today between Jews, Christians, and Moslems, and between Jews and Arabs, is a painful reminder that Jerusalem, whose very name means city of peace, is far from that. It is easy for the ordinary believer to become resigned to the seemingly unsolvable, complex religious and political tensions that pervade this holy place. We ought to continue to pray that some day peace will return to this city and that it will become a place where believers from the three Abrahamic religions can live together in peace. Beyond that, it is very helpful for Christians to work without ceasing to come to a deeper understanding of Jews and Moslems. What better way of doing this than to form relationships with fellow monotheistic believers, relationships founded on mutual respect, openness, trust, and, most of all, love. In your own community what can you do to build bridges and to foster understanding, and thus to promote peace?

Jesus' Authority Questioned and Parable of the Tenant Farmers (20:1–19)

20:1 One day as he was teaching the people in the temple area and proclaiming the good news, the chief priests and scribes, together with the elders, approached him 2and said to him, "Tell us, by what authority are you doing these things? Or who is the one who gave you this authority?" 3He said to them in reply, "I shall ask you a question. Tell me, 4was John's baptism of heavenly or of human origin?" 5They discussed this among themselves, and said, "If we say, 'Of heavenly origin,' he will say, 'Why did you not believe him?' ⁶But if we say, 'Of human origin,' then all the people will stone us, for they are convinced that John was a prophet." ⁷ So they answered that they did not know from where it came. ⁸Then Jesus said to them, "Neither shall I tell you by what authority I do these things."

⁹ Then he proceeded to tell the people this parable. "(A) man planted a vineyard, leased it to tenant farmers, and then went on a journey for a long time. ¹⁰At harvest time he sent a servant to the tenant farmers to receive some of the produce of the vineyard. But they beat the servant and sent him away empty-handed. ¹¹ So he proceeded to send another servant, but him also they beat and insulted and sent away empty-handed. ¹²Then he proceeded to send a third, but this one too they wounded and threw out. ¹³ The owner of the vineyard said, 'What shall I do? I shall send my beloved son; maybe they will respect him.' ¹⁴But when the tenant farmers saw him they said to one another, 'This is the heir. Let us kill him that the inheritance may become ours.' ¹⁵ So they threw him out of the vineyard and killed him. What will the owner of the vineyard do to them? ¹⁶ He will come and put those tenant farmers to death and turn over the vineyard to others." When the people heard this, they exclaimed, "Let it not be so!" ¹⁷But he looked at them and asked, "What then does this scripture passage mean:

'The stone which the builders rejected
has become the cornerstone'?

¹⁸ Everyone who falls on that stone will be dashed to pieces; and it will crush anyone on whom it falls." ¹⁹The scribes and chief priests sought to lay their hands on him at that very hour, but they feared the people, for they knew that he had addressed this parable to them.

Ever faithful to his mission, Jesus continues to teach the good news to the people (see 4:18, 43; 8:1), even as the opposition intensifies. The Temple area, the most sacred place for the Jews, is the arena for Jesus' saving instruction about God's plan for them. While the people are receptive to his teaching, the chief priest, scribes, and elders ask challenging questions with hostile intent. In this scene Jesus' opponents attempt to undermine his popularity by calling into question the source of his authority.

Jesus skillfully escapes the traps of those who would incriminate and embarrass him by giving impressive responses. He answers their questions with counter-questions that cause them to re-evaluate their rejection of John the Baptist. Both John and Jesus were sent by God to call the people to repentance and conversion of heart. If the Jerusalem leaders acknowledge that John's authority comes from God, then so does Jesus'. If they dismiss John's baptism as being a human machination, then they put their own lives at risk. Unwilling to commit themselves, they receive no answers from Jesus to their questions.

Turning his attention to the people, with the opponents still on the scene, Jesus uses this occasion to teach about the source of his authority. He interprets his role and that of his opponents by telling a story involving an absentee landlord and tenants who revolt. This parable is an allegory—the main players symbolize characters in the divine drama of salvation. The landowner represents God, and the vineyard symbolizes Israel (see Is 5:1–7). The servants stand for the messengers God has graciously sent to the people. These messengers are the prophets who have been persecuted and rejected by unrighteous leaders—represented by the tenant farmers.

The landowner's son is, of course, Jesus, God's beloved. "My beloved son" (20:13) clearly evokes the divine words spoken to Jesus at his baptism (3:22). The flashback to this event fully illuminates the source of Jesus' authority. In sending his son the owner makes one last attempt hoping that his directives will be heard and respected. Ironically, because the messenger was the owner's son and heir, the tenants killed him outside the vineyard—an allusion to Jesus' death outside the city walls. A second irony is that by plotting to seize the inheritance for themselves, the tenants risked forfeiting their call to become heirs to the kingdom Jesus proclaimed.

The others to whom the vineyard was given represent those who respond to Jesus' teaching. However, this interpretation is problematic since the people respond: "Let it not be so!" Hence, some suggest that "others" refers to the Roman troops who capture Jerusalem.

As an interpretative key to this story, Jesus cites Psalm 118:22 about the rejected stone (see 19:38 where this same psalm is quoted). Rejected by the leaders (see 9:22), God's son is vindicated: he becomes the cornerstone of the new building, reconstructed Israel. Thus, Jesus replaces what the Temple symbolizes. The stone that was seen as useless becomes the stone than endures. This stone will bring the demise of those who trip over it as an obstacle (20:18). Shaken by Jesus' defense of his authority in this story, the scribes and chief priests seek to do what the tenant farmers did, that is lay hands on Jesus and bring about his death. However, their fear of the people prevented them from doing so.

For reflection: The question of authority challenges us in several ways. On a personal level there is our inner authority, the power to speak and to act based upon our own convictions. The depth of our faith, integration of values, and strength of character give us the kind of authority that can be used as a force for good in our family and community. Jesus' words and deeds exemplify the kind of authority that is life-giving. Grounded in his relationship with God, Jesus speaks with a clarity that illuminates his saving role in the vineyard of God's people.

What kind of authority does Jesus have in our life? Is the authority with which we speak and act grounded in our relationship with God's beloved son? Or, is our behavior determined by a desire to please others or to gain acceptance? If our intention to embrace the Gospel does not cost us anything, perhaps we have not really accepted God's messengers or Jesus, God's prophet.

The Question about the Resurrection (20:27–40)

[27]Some Sadducees, those who deny that there is a resurrection, came forward and put this question to him, [28]saying, "Teacher, Moses wrote for us, 'If someone's brother dies leaving a wife but no child, his brother must take the wife and raise up descendants for his brother.' [29]Now there were seven brothers; the first married a woman but died childless. [30]Then the second [31]and the third married her, and likewise all the seven died childless. [32]Finally the woman also died. [33]Now at the resurrection whose wife will that woman be? For all seven had been married to her." [34]Jesus said to them, "The children of this age marry and remarry; [35]but those who are deemed worthy to attain to the coming age and to the resurrection of the dead neither marry nor are given in marriage. [36]They can no longer die, for they are like angels; and they are the children of God because they are the ones who will rise. [37]That the dead will rise even Moses made known in the passage about the bush, when he called 'Lord' the God of Abraham, the God of Isaac, and the God of Jacob; [38]and he is not God of the dead, but of the living, for to him all are alive." [39]Some of the scribes said in reply, "Teacher, you have answered well." [40]And they no longer dared to ask him anything.

Before this passage the scribes and Pharisees send spies to trap Jesus with a tax question (20:20–26). Amazed by his reply, they are reduced to silence. Jesus acknowledges that allegiance is to be paid to Caesar whose image is carried on the coin of the realm. He insists, however, that primary allegiance is owed to God whose image humanity bears (see Gn 1:27). This encounter prepares for the trial scene when the people distort Jesus' response and charge him with opposing tax payment to Caesar (23:2).

The next group to take on Jesus are the Sadducees who attempt to entangle him in a dispute about the resurrection. Well aware of Levirate marriage legislation about perpetuating the family of a man who dies childless (Dt 25:5–10), the Sadducees pose a perplexing question. Jesus rejects the premise of their question: he counters that the exclusive bond of marriage does not apply in resurrected life. Using multiple arguments Jesus demonstrates how radically different life is for the children of God in the kingdom.

Jesus argues from immortality: "they can no longer die" (see 2 Ma 7); from comparison: "they are like angels"; and from scripture: "that the dead will rise even Moses made known." The reference to angels is a subtle dig at the Sadducees for they did not believe in these heavenly beings. The scriptural argument, based on the Pentateuch (first five books of the Bible)—held to be authoritative by the Sadducees—receives the most emphasis. Since God is the God of the living and not of the dead, then the patriarchs, Abraham, Isaac, and Jacob, who are bound to God in a covenantal relationship (see Ex 3:2, 5, 15), must themselves be still living. How is this possible? Because God has extended to them life after death by means of the resurrection.

In continuity with the teaching of the Pharisees (Acts 23:6–10), Jesus' answer pleases the scribes, who for once do not oppose him. Life for the children of God in the kingdom will be radically different—it will be life that will not end. Hence there is no need for marriage or human propagation to continue. This does not mean, however, that deep human relationships founded on love will not in some way endure. Since God is the God of the living, since we are God's children and since love does not end—as Paul attests (1 Cor 13:13)—God will raise up to a radically new and transformed existence those who trust in him.

For reflection: Important to Pharisaic Judaism and central to Christianity is belief in the resurrection of the dead (see Dn

180

12:1–3). Those who seek to know the details of resurrected existence are hard pressed to find in the scriptures—either Old or New Testament—elaborate descriptions of any sort. Negatively put, resurrected life will be an absence of pain and hunger for the poor, of persecution and rejection for disciples, and of suffering and death for all. The resurrected will no longer walk in shadow of death or fear any evil (Ps 22:4). On the positive side, life in the kingdom will be an undiminished experience of God with Christ, the life-giving Spirit (1 Cor 15:45).

In the blessed resurrection believers will be with the Lord forever (1 Thes 4:17), will share the very life of God, and will see with brilliant clarity the Lord's goodness (Ps 26:13). The heavenly kingdom is the "place" of our real citizenship (Phil 3:20) and everlasting home (2 Cor 5:1). Belief in the resurrection of the dead is a central part of the Christian creed. Reflect for a moment what place the resurrection has in your personal creed. What do you believe about the resurrection and how does this impact your faith?

Jesus' Eschatological Discourse (21:5–36)

Luke sets the scene for Jesus' extended discourse about end-time events by briefly placing on center stage a poor widow (21:1–4). Jesus observes that she gave her whole livelihood, putting it into the Temple treasury. She thus becomes another compelling example of a poor person who detached herself from everything, a sign of her total dependence on God the source of all.

> [5] While some people were speaking about how the temple was adorned with costly stones and votive offerings, he said, [6] "All that you see here— the days will come when there will not be left a stone upon another stone that will not be thrown down."
> [7] Then they asked him, "Teacher, when will this happen? And what sign will there be when all these things are about to

happen?" [8] He answered, "See that you not be deceived, for many will come in my name, saying, 'I am he,' and 'The time has come.' Do not follow them! [9] When you hear of wars and insurrections, do not be terrified; for such things must happen first, but it will not immediately be the end." [10] Then he said to them, "Nation will rise against nation, and kingdom against kingdom. [11] There will be powerful earthquakes, famines, and plagues from place to place; and awesome sights and mighty signs will come from the sky.

[12] "Before all this happens, however, they will seize and persecute you, they will hand you over to the synagogues and to prisons, and they will have you led before kings and governors because of my name. [13] It will lead to your giving testimony. [14] Remember, you are not to prepare your defense beforehand, [15] for I myself shall give you a wisdom in speaking that all your adversaries will be powerless to resist or refute. [16] You will even be handed over by parents, brothers, relatives, and friends, and they will put some of you to death. [17] You will be hated by all because of my name, [18] but not a hair on your head will be destroyed. [19] By your perseverance you will secure your lives.

[20] "When you see Jerusalem surrounded by armies, know that its desolation is at hand. [21] Then those in Judea must flee to the mountains. Let those within the city escape from it, and let those in the countryside not enter the city, [22] for these days are the time of punishment when all the scriptures are fulfilled. [23] Woe to pregnant women and nursing mothers in those days, for a terrible calamity will come upon the earth and a wrathful judgment upon this people. [24] They will fall by the edge of the sword and be taken as captives to all the Gentiles; and Jerusalem will be trampled underfoot by the Gentiles until the times of the Gentiles are fulfilled.

[25] "There will be signs in the sun, the moon, and the stars, and on earth nations will be in dismay, perplexed by the roaring of the sea and the waves. [26] People will die of fright in anticipation of what is coming upon the world, for the powers of the heavens will be shaken. [27] And then they will see the

Son of Man coming in a cloud with power and great glory. [28] But when these signs begin to happen, stand erect and raise your heads because your redemption is at hand."

[29] He taught them a lesson. "Consider the fig tree and all the other trees. [30] When their buds burst open, you see for yourselves and know that summer is now near; [31] in the same way, when you see these things happening, know that the kingdom of God is near. [32] Amen, I say to you, this generation will not pass away until all these things have taken place. [33] Heaven and earth will pass away, but my words will not pass away.

[34] "Beware that your hearts do not become drowsy from carousing and drunkenness and the anxieties of daily life, and that day catch you by surprise [35] like a trap. For that day will assault everyone who lives on the face of the earth. [36] Be vigilant at all times and pray that you have the strength to escape the tribulations that are imminent and to stand before the Son of Man."

Throughout the ages many interpreters have been misled in reading this passage, culling through the details attempting to relate them to historical events of the past and to establish a timetable for future happenings. This approach, however, widely misses the mark of Luke's intent. The purpose of this extended passage is to offer hope and encouragement during times of persecution, and to assure the faithful that the future coming of the Son of Man will bring the fullness of redemption.

There are four main sections: the first addresses the times immediately before the destruction of the Temple (21:5–11), the second sketches the expected persecution of the disciples that will take place before the events just mentioned (21:12–19), the third predicts the destruction of Jerusalem, the city of the Temple (21:20–24), and the final section focuses on the future coming of the Son of Man at the end (21:25–36). Luke presents Jesus as a prophet who foretells the future. Since the first three of these episodes had already taken place when Luke wrote his Gospel, namely the persecution of the disciples, the destruction of the Temple, and the fall of Jerusalem, Luke assures his readers that the words of this prophet can be forever trusted (21:33). This builds confidence in his final words about the future coming of the Son of Man when God's definitive rule will be established.

There will be persecution for the disciples. Just as Jesus will be handed over (9:44; 18:32; 24:7), so also will his followers (21:12; see Acts 4:3; 5:18; 12:1; 21:27). Jesus has met controversy in his ministry. The disciples can expect no less. The reference to synagogues, kings and governors suggests that they will be brought before both Jewish and Roman authorities. Paul is a prime example of one who had to confront both groups (see Acts 24–26). The disciples are not to prepare their defense, for Jesus will give them the wisdom necessary to confront their opponents. This recalls 12:12 where the Holy Spirit is promised as their teacher. When given a chance they are to testify before their adversaries as Stephen and Paul will do so boldly in Acts (Acts 7; 21–26). Even though the disciples will be hated and put to death, they are to persevere.

Luke's vivid description of the fall of Jerusalem indicates that he was well aware of the siege of this city and its destruction by the Romans in 70 C.E. God uses the Gentiles to punish the unfaithful inhabitants, unable to escape. The elusive phrase "until the times of the Gentiles are fulfilled" probably refers to the eventual restoration of Jerusalem (see Zec 12:10).

As desperate as things seem, the promise of the future coming of the Son of Man offers hope. In contrast to those who die of fright because their concerns tie them to this world, faithful disciples will be able to stand erect with their head held high constantly alert to greet Jesus, the Son of Man. At his coming redemption (*lytrōsis*, see 1:68; 2:38; 24:21; Acts 7:35) will be at hand for Jerusalem and its inhabitants. This passage concludes with similar words of encouragement. Those disciples who remain vigilant at all times, and pray for the strength of perseverance, will have nothing to fear.

For reflection: In every generation one could easily relate many world events to the "signs" in this passage: armies of destruction, powerful earthquakes, devastating famines, and cosmic occurrences—one might think here of the depleting ozone or ecological disasters, e.g., oil spills and the depletion of the rain forest. Such events can prompt even staunch believers to feel hopeless and helpless, to search in vain for meaning, to wonder whether ultimate redemption is possible, or simply to doubt that God cares.

A fearful response leads to paralysis and despair. This passage calls us to be people of courage, possessing a strength that is grounded not in our own power but in the promise of God's prophet to be with us. Our response is to be open to the divine wisdom that is made available to us in the Spirit, and to allow that wisdom to guide our responses. What wisdom have you been given, and how have you used this to make a faithful response to the challenges at hand?

VII

Passion Narrative and Resurrection Stories
(22:1–24:53)

Even before the first Gospel was written the followers of Jesus began to tell the Passion Narrative, the story of his final days. This addresses one of the most perplexing challenges they faced. How were they to understand for themselves and to explain to others that this Jesus in whom they believed was Lord and Messiah, yet had suffered such a dishonorable death, and this on two accounts. First, he was sentenced to death by crucifixion—the Roman form of capital punishment—and executed with two other condemned criminals. Secondly, having hung on a cross he was considered by the Torah to be cursed by God (Dt 21:23). Thus, from both a Roman and a Jewish perspective he would seem to be the most unlikely person to be acclaimed as a life-giving Spirit and worshiped as the Son of God. The passion narrative is a compelling effort to address these issues.

Unlike in the previous chapters, the entire text of the passion will be presented followed by a brief commentary. Since a close reading of this narrative is itself a meditation, the reader is encouraged to allow the text to speak in a way that is personally meaningful. To honor this process we will not add our own meditative reflections.

Inseparably connected to the passion story are the resurrection narratives. Our focus will be on the Emmaus episode, one of the most engaging and theologically rich of all the Lukan narratives.

The Plot and the Preparations for the Passover (22:1–13)

22:1 Now the feast of Unleavened Bread, called the Passover, was drawing near, 2 and the chief priests and the scribes were seeking a way to put him to death, for they were afraid of the people. 3 Then Satan entered into Judas, the one surnamed Iscariot, who was counted among the Twelve, 4 and he went to the chief priests and temple guards to discuss a plan for handing him over to them. 5 They were pleased and agreed to pay him money. 6 He accepted their offer and sought a favorable opportunity to hand him over to them in the absence of a crowd.

7 When the day of the feast of Unleavened Bread arrived, the day for sacrificing the Passover lamb, 8 he sent out Peter and John, instructing them, "Go and make preparations for us to eat the Passover." 9 They asked him, "Where do you want us to make the preparations?" 10 And he answered them, "When you go into the city, a man will meet you carrying a jar of water. Follow him into the house that he enters 11 and say to the master of the house, 'The teacher says to you, "Where is the guest room where I may eat the Passover with my disciples?" ' 12 He will show you a large upper room that is furnished. Make the preparations there." 13 Then they went off and found everything exactly as he had told them, and there they prepared the Passover.

Relentless in their determination to eliminate Jesus, the religious leaders find an accomplice in Judas, one of the Twelve. Becoming one of those disciples not able to withstand being sifted like wheat (22:31), Judas succumbs to the power of darkness (22:53), personified in Satan. Absent since the temptation of Jesus (4:13), Satan comes on the scene again when he enters one of those from Jesus' inner circle. Under Satan's influence, Judas hatches a plot to hand over Jesus, a plot that will soon succeed (22:47–53). Luke in no way diminishes the perfidy of Judas, for at the beginning of Acts he recounts his ignominious end (Acts 1:15–26). The demise of Judas recalls Simeon's prophecy at the beginning of the Gospel, that Jesus is destined for the rise and fall of many (2:34).

In no way a victim to the ominous circumstances that are rapidly unfolding, Jesus takes decisive action in planning for the Passover. He sends Peter and John to make preparations in the "guest room," which translates *kataluma*, the same Greek word that is rendered "inn" in 2:7. Neither as an infant coming into the world nor as an adult about to depart from his disciples does Jesus have a place of his own. Contrary to the image of Leonardo Da Vinci's famous painting of the Last Supper portraying Jesus with the Twelve, in Luke a wider community of disciples beyond the Twelve joins Jesus for the Passover (see 22:11, 32, 39, 45, where "brothers" means disciples). This group of disciples could well include several of the those who have followed Jesus, both men and women. If so, they are the ones gathered in the large upper room where Jesus shared the cup and broke the bread.

Last Supper (22:14–23)

[14] When the hour came, he took his place at table with the apostles. [15] He said to them, "I have eagerly desired to eat this Passover with you before I suffer, [16] for, I tell you, I shall not eat it [again] until there is fulfillment in the kingdom of God." [17] Then he took a cup, gave thanks, and said, "Take this and share it among yourselves; [18] for I tell you [that] from this time on I shall not drink of the fruit of the vine until the kingdom of God comes." [19] Then he took the bread, said the blessing, broke it, and gave it to them, saying, "This is my body, which will be given for you; do this in memory of me." [20] And likewise the cup after they had eaten, saying, "This cup is the new covenant in my blood, which will be shed for you.

[21] "And yet behold, the hand of the one who is to betray me is with me on the table; [22] for the Son of Man indeed goes as it has been determined; but woe to that man by whom he is

betrayed." [23] And they began to debate among themselves who among them would do such a deed.

This supper stands out from among several previous fellowship meals with Jesus (5:27–32; 7:31–34; 15:1–2; 19:7). The appointed hour and the Passover setting give this repast special significance. The hour refers to Jesus' exodus, meaning his death, resurrection, and return to God. The Passover is a solemn ritual that commemorates God's past liberation of the Israelites from the slavery of Egypt as well as anticipates God's final saving action in the future. Jesus expressly reinterprets this sacred meal in terms of a new covenant sealed with his own blood that will be poured out for the disciples (see Ex 24:3–8; Jer 31:31–34).

Jesus' fourfold action of taking, blessing, breaking, and giving the bread recalls the feeding of the five thousand (9:16) and points ahead to the recognition meal at Emmaus (24:30). He interprets the bread as his *sōma*, meaning not just his physical body but his whole human person. The giving of his *sōma* has salvific meaning, and is an action to be repeated. Jesus himself takes a vow to abstain from participating in the meal until the coming of the kingdom of God (22:16,18). Either this means the time after his death and resurrection when he will be present in the eucharistic gatherings of the community (24:30; Acts 2:42–47), or it refers to the eschatological banquet when the Son of Man returns (see 13:29; 14:15–24).

The bond of unity manifested by the shared cup and blessed bread is shattered by the intention of the betrayer whose presence at the table is announced by Jesus. This startling disclosure sparks a debate among the participants, and leads to an argument about who among them ranks at the top.

Jesus' Farewell Discourse (22:24–38)

[24] Then an argument broke out among them about which of them should be regarded as the greatest. [25] He said to them,

"The kings of the Gentiles lord it over them and those in authority over them are addressed as 'Benefactors'; [26] but among you it shall not be so. Rather, let the greatest among you be as the youngest, and the leader as the servant. [27] For who is greater: the one seated at table or the one who serves? Is it not the one seated at table? I am among you as the one who serves. [28] It is you who have stood by me in my trials; [29] and I confer a kingdom on you, just as my Father has conferred one on me, [30] that you may eat and drink at my table in my kingdom; and you will sit on thrones judging the twelve tribes of Israel.

[31] "Simon, Simon, behold Satan has demanded to sift all of you like wheat, [32] but I have prayed that your own faith may not fail; and once you have turned back, you must strengthen your brothers." [33] He said to him, "Lord, I am prepared to go to prison and to die with you." [34] But he replied, "I tell you, Peter, before the cock crows this day, you will deny three times that you know me."

[35] He said to them, "When I sent you forth without a money bag or a sack or sandals, were you in need of anything?" "No, nothing," they replied. [36] He said to them, "But now one who has a money bag should take it, and likewise a sack, and one who does not have a sword should sell his cloak and buy one. [37] For I tell you that this scripture must be fulfilled in me, namely, 'He was counted among the wicked'; and indeed what is written about me is coming to fulfillment." [38] Then they said, "Lord, look, there are two swords here." But he replied, "It is enough!"

It is common in ancient Greek and Jewish traditions for an honored person near death to address family and friends about his past life, to give encouragement and instruction about the future, to establish a new leader and to give directions about how that leadership is to be exercised. Examples include Jacob (Gn 49:1–27), Moses (Dt 31), and Paul (Acts 20:17–35). Jesus reflects on the royal authority that the Father has given to him (see 19:11–27, 38), an authority that he used to serve and not to lord over his disciples. Though endowed as king, Jesus also recalls that he has not been without trials of his own.

After chastising the disciples for acting like Gentile kings in arguing about who is the greatest (see 9:46–48), Jesus offers a radically new paradigm for exercising authority. He teaches that as leaders the greatest is to be as the youngest and is to serve rather than be served. Only then does Jesus confer upon them the authority to judge the twelve tribes of Israel, meaning that they are to be the leaders of God's reconstituted people, a role they carry out in the early church (see Acts 1–6).

Simon's boldness in pledging to die with his master is severely tempered by Jesus who tells the first among the apostles of his imminent betrayal. Still, Jesus prays for him, and discloses that Simon will turn back. Because he does experience first hand a humiliating failure, he can understand others who are overcome by their own cowardness and weakness. Perhaps it is for this reason that Jesus singles out Simon for the role of strengthening his brothers.

The Agony in the Garden and the Betrayal of Jesus (22:39–53)

³⁹Then going out he went, as was his custom, to the Mount of Olives, and the disciples followed him. ⁴⁰When he arrived at the place he said to them, "Pray that you may not undergo the test." ⁴¹After withdrawing about a stone's throw from them and kneeling, he prayed, ⁴²saying, "Father, if you are willing, take this cup away from me; still, not my will but yours be done." ⁴³[And to strengthen him an angel from heaven appeared to him. ⁴⁴He was in such agony and he prayed so fervently that his sweat became like drops of blood falling on the ground.] ⁴⁵When he rose from prayer and returned to his disciples, he found them sleeping from grief. ⁴⁶He said to them, "Why are you sleeping? Get up and pray that you may not undergo the test."

⁴⁷ While he was still speaking, a crowd approached and in front was one of the Twelve, a man named Judas. He went up to Jesus to kiss him. ⁴⁸ Jesus said to him, "Judas, are you betraying the Son of Man with a kiss?" ⁴⁹ His disciples realized what was about to happen, and they asked, "Lord, shall we strike with a sword?" ⁵⁰ And one of them struck the high priest's servant and cut off his right ear. ⁵¹ But Jesus said in reply, "Stop, no more of this!" Then he touched the servant's ear and healed him. ⁵² And Jesus said to the chief priests and temple guards and elders who had come for him, "Have you come out as against a robber, with swords and clubs? ⁵³ Day after day I was with you in the temple area, and you did not seize me; but this is your hour, the time for the power of darkness."

Though accompanied by his disciples to a place where they had often gathered, Jesus is very much alone. While he prays they sleep. Then Judas, one of his own, leads a hostile crowd to arrest him. And finally, one of the disciples confronts the opposition with an act of violence. Yet, Jesus responds with an act of healing. Before and after his prayer Jesus instructs his disciples to pray that they may not undergo the test (22:40, 46). Crippled by their own *lupē* (grief, sorrow) they are unable to stay awake as Jesus had previously instructed them (see 21:36). Greco-Roman writers described *lupē* as a debilitating fear in the face of conflict, depleting one's strength.

Vigilant in prayer before the Father, Jesus discloses his vulnerability. He would prefer not to be put to this final test (see 11:4), that is to accept the cup, a symbol of the pouring out of his life through suffering and death. However, not without an anguishing interior struggle, Jesus aligns his will with that of his Father. In his trial an angel from heaven strengthens him. The imagery of *agonia* (agony, struggle) and the perfuse sweating of blood portrays Jesus as a moral athlete seeking victory in a fateful contest against the powers of darkness. In spite of whatever interior turmoil he faced, Jesus remains resolute, faithfully obedient to the divine plan.

Without the human support of his disciples, he is betrayed by a trusted friend through a kiss, a gesture of affection (see 7:45; 15:20). Addressing the traitor by name, Jesus asks a question replete with irony. To paraphrase: "Judas, how is it that you use a sign of intimacy for a sign of treachery?" Rising to Jesus' defense another misguided disciple draws his sword and strikes a blow (22:50, see 22:35–38). Not to be drawn into the politics of violence, Jesus becomes an agent of healing, putting into practice love of enemy (6:27–36). Remaining steady and centered throughout the chaos of this scene, Jesus challenges though does not resist the hostile action of those who came under cover of darkness to arrest him.

Peter's Denial of Jesus and Jesus before the Sanhedrin (22:54–71)

[54] After arresting him they led him away and took him into the house of the high priest; Peter was following at a distance. [55] They lit a fire in the middle of the courtyard and sat around it, and Peter sat down with them. [56] When a maid saw him seated in the light, she looked intently at him and said, "This man too was with him." [57] But he denied it saying, "Woman, I do not know him." [58] A short while later someone else saw him and said, "You too are one of them"; but Peter answered, "My friend, I am not." [59] About an hour later, still another insisted, "Assuredly, this man too was with him, for he also is a Galilean." [60] But Peter said, "My friend, I do not know what you are talking about." Just as he was saying this, the cock crowed, [61] and the Lord turned and looked at Peter; and Peter remembered the word of the Lord, how he had said to him, "Before the cock crows today, you will deny me three times." [62] He went out and began to weep bitterly. [63] The men who held Jesus in custody were ridiculing and beating him. [64] They blindfolded him and questioned him, saying, "Prophesy! Who is it that struck you?" [65] And they reviled him in saying many other things against him.

⁶⁶ When day came the council of elders of the people met, both chief priests and scribes, and they brought him before their Sanhedrin. ⁶⁷ They said, "If you are the Messiah, tell us," but he replied to them, "If I tell you, you will not believe, ⁶⁸ and if I question, you will not respond. ⁶⁹ But from this time on the Son of Man will be seated at the right hand of the power of God." ⁷⁰ They all asked, "Are you then the Son of God?" He replied to them, "You say that I am." ⁷¹ Then they said, "What further need have we for testimony? We have heard it from his own mouth."

While Jesus was led away as a prisoner Peter is given three opportunities to claim his allegiance to the one who once called him to be a fisher of humans (5:10). Evidently overcome by his own fear, Peter repeatedly denies any relationship with Jesus. In doing so he shows the emptiness of his own boast at the Last Supper (22:33) and places himself at risk of being denied before the angels of God (12:9). Yet, Peter was not completely turned in upon himself, for he caught the Lord's glance—a glance that triggered his memory. By remembering the word of God's prophet (22:34; see 24:8), he began his own spiritual conversion. His interior repentance was publicly expressed by his bitter weeping.

Meanwhile Jesus is mocked and beaten. Blindfolded by those who were themselves blinded to his true identity, Jesus was asked to play the prophet. What supreme irony! For the reader knows that Jesus is indeed the prophet who has already predicted his mockery (18:32), his betrayal (22:21–22), and his denial (22:34).

Before the whole Jesus allows their questions to stand as testimony to him. By asking whether he is the Messiah (see 2:11; 23:35; Acts 2:31) and the Son of God (1:32, 35; 3:22; 4:3, 9, 41; 8:28; 9:35), the entire leadership of this official ruling body unwittingly convey his true identity. Jesus' unwavering presence and penetrating responses serve as a powerful witness that he is truly who they say he is. In this way he also becomes a model for those early church leaders such as Peter (Acts 3–5), Stephen (Acts 6–7), and Paul (Acts 21–26), who will be called to testify to their faith.

Jesus before Herod and Pilate (23:1–16)

23:1 Then the whole assembly of them arose and brought him before Pilate. ²They brought charges against him, saying, "We found this man misleading our people; he opposes the payment of taxes to Caesar and maintains that he is the Messiah, a king." ³Pilate asked him, "Are you the king of the Jews?" He said to him in reply, "You say so." ⁴Pilate then addressed the chief priests and the crowds, "I find this man not guilty." ⁵But they were adamant and said, "He is inciting the people with his teaching throughout all Judea, from Galilee where he began even to here."

⁶On hearing this Pilate asked if the man was a Galilean; ⁷and upon learning that he was under Herod's jurisdiction, he sent him to Herod who was in Jerusalem at that time. ⁸Herod was very glad to see Jesus; he had been wanting to see him for a long time, for he had heard about him and had been hoping to see him perform some sign. ⁹He questioned him at length, but he gave him no answer. ¹⁰The chief priests and scribes, meanwhile, stood by accusing him harshly. ¹¹[Even] Herod and his soldiers treated him contemptuously and mocked him, and after clothing him in resplendent garb, he sent him back to Pilate. ¹²Herod and Pilate became friends that very day, even though they had been enemies formerly. ¹³Pilate then summoned the chief priests, the rulers, and the people ¹⁴and said to them, "You brought this man to me and accused him of inciting the people to revolt. I have conducted my investigation in your presence and have not found this man guilty of the charges you have brought against him, ¹⁵nor did Herod, for he sent him back to us. So no capital crime has been committed by him. ¹⁶Therefore I shall have him flogged and then release him." [17]

The entire Sanhedrin, the Jewish governing body, brought Jesus before Pilate, the Roman prefect, thus fulfilling the prophecy that he would be delivered to the Gentiles (18:32). They accused Jesus of misleading the people and supported the case with two specific charges: opposing payment of taxes to Caesar and claiming to be the Messiah. The first is patently false (see 20:20–26), and the second lacked clear evidence (see 22:66–71). After questioning Jesus (23:3) and conducting a thorough investigation in what seems to be a formal trial (23:14–15), Pilate declares Jesus to be innocent (23:4,14), a judgment confirmed by Herod (23:15). When Jesus appears before Pilate a second time, he emphatically rules that Jesus is not guilty of the charges brought against him (23:22). Luke's point is clear: before Roman authorities Jesus is innocent. Members of the religious leadership and some of the people in Jerusalem persistently press their case and finally force Pilate's hand (23:1–5, 10, 13, 18, 21, 23–25).

When Pilate learns that Jesus is a Galilean, he sends him to Herod, who for some time had been perplexed about Jesus (9:7–9, see 3:1, 19–20; 13:31–35). Glad to see Jesus, Herod is hoping to see a miracle ("see" is used three times in 23:8). His idle curiosity, however, falls far short of what is required: faith in Jesus (7:50; 8:48, 50; 17:19; 23:35, 47–49). Like the innocently suffering righteous one of Isaiah 53:7, Jesus responds with silence, modeling a different response from his prior instruction to the disciples about speaking words the Holy Spirit gives them (12:11–12; 21:14–15; see Paul in Acts 22–26). Disappointed in his quest for some miracle, Herod and his soldiers publicly dishonor Jesus by treating him with contempt and mocking him (23:11). In their opposition to Jesus, Pilate and Herod form a friendship—more sinister than praiseworthy—that unites them against the Messiah (see Acts 4:26–27).

Sentence to Death and the Way of the Cross (23:18–32)

[18] But all together they shouted out, "Away with this man! Release Barabbas to us." [19] (Now Barabbas had been imprisoned for a rebellion that had taken place in the city and for murder.) [20] Again Pilate addressed them, still wishing to release Jesus, [21] but they continued their shouting, "Crucify him! Crucify him!" [22] Pilate addressed them a third time, "What evil has this man done? I found him guilty of no capital crime. Therefore I shall have him flogged and then release him." [23] With loud shouts, however, they persisted in calling for his crucifixion, and their voices prevailed. [24] The verdict of Pilate was that their demand should be granted. [25] So he released the man who had been imprisoned for rebellion and murder, for whom they asked, and he handed Jesus over to them to deal with as they wished.

[26] As they led him away they took hold of a certain Simon, a Cyrenian, who was coming in from the country; and after laying the cross on him, they made him carry it behind Jesus. [27] A large crowd of people followed Jesus, including many women who mourned and lamented him. [28] Jesus turned to them and said, "Daughters of Jerusalem, do not weep for me; weep instead for yourselves and for your children, [29] for indeed, the days are coming when people will say, 'Blessed are the barren, the wombs that never bore and the breasts that never nursed.' [30] At that time people will say to the mountains, 'Fall upon us!' and to the hills, 'Cover us!' [31] for if these things are done when the wood is green what will happen when it is dry?" [32] Now two others, both criminals, were led away with him to be executed.

The people who charge Jesus with insurrection now in supreme irony lobby to have Barabbas, a convicted insurrectionist, released. Note that the verse about the practice of freeing a prisoner at festival time is not part of the original text (23:17). Barabbas, a name meaning "son of the father," has dishonored his father by his criminal activity, while Jesus, the

Father's son (see 2:49; 10:21–22; 11:2; 22:29, 42), remains faithful to the end. Ever true to his mission Jesus maintains his inner freedom even as he stands in place of the prisoner who is released.

In a shouting frenzy the crowd prevails upon Pilate to hand Jesus over. Under pressure Pilate abandons his convictions and acts as a coward, sacrificing individual justice for political expedience. Casting aside the opportunity for heroic action, he becomes a tragic figure. With Jesus in their control, they—either the crowd or the Roman soldiers (the text is not clear)—lead him away (23:26). They make Simon, a man from Cyrene in North Africa, carry Jesus' cross and follow after him. His action is a literal reminder of Jesus' call to discipleship (9:23; 14:27). A large crowd of people along with many women also follow in the footsteps of the prophet. Jesus redirects the mourning of the daughters of Jerusalem (see Is 37:22; 52:2; 62:11; Zep 3:14; Zec 9:9) from him to the children of Jerusalem, a city destined for destruction, since it resists what makes for peace (13:34–35; 19:41–44; 21:20–24). The startling beatitude praising barren women reverses the oracle of salvation where Jerusalem is promised many children (23:29, see Is 49:19–21; 54:1).

The Crucifixion (23:33–43)

[33]When they came to the place called the Skull, they crucified him and the criminals there, one on his right, the other on his left. [34] [Then Jesus said, "Father, forgive them, they know not what they do."] They divided his garments by casting lots. [35] The people stood by and watched; the rulers, meanwhile, sneered at him and said, "He saved others, let him save himself if he is the chosen one, the Messiah of God." [36]Even the soldiers jeered at him. As they approached to offer him wine [37] they called out, "If you are King of the Jews, save yourself." [38] Above him there was an inscription that read, "This is the King of the Jews."

³⁹ Now one of the criminals hanging there reviled Jesus, saying, "Are you not the Messiah? Save yourself and us." ⁴⁰The other, however, rebuking him, said in reply, "Have you no fear of God, for you are subject to the same condemnation? ⁴¹ And indeed, we have been condemned justly, for the sentence we received corresponds to our crimes, but this man has done nothing criminal." ⁴² Then he said, "Jesus, remember me when you come into your kingdom." ⁴³ He replied to him, "Amen, I say to you, today you will be with me in Paradise."

Put to death between two criminals, Jesus fulfills the prophecy from scripture he had previously quoted (22:37). Though suffering physical torment on the cross, Jesus asks the Father to extend God's mercy to those who rejected him. In doing so, he follows his own counsel of praying for those who mistreat him (see 6:28), as he prayed for Peter who was about to deny him (22:31–34). In his dying moment Jesus lives out his mission of calling sinners to repentance (see 5:32) by assuring them of the Father's bountiful forgiveness. Evidently touched by this prayer, the people who had pressed for Jesus' execution, now begin to experience a change of heart as they stood by and watched. After Jesus' death they will return home beating their breast (23:48; see 18:13), an expression of remorse and a sign of conversion.

Recalling Peter's threefold denial, the narrator tells of Jesus being mocked three times: by some religious leaders, by the Roman soldiers, and finally by the non-repentant criminal. In fulfillment of Psalms 22:7–8, they mock Jesus as the Messiah of God and the King of the Jews, taunting him to save himself. Adding to the high drama, the soldiers in their own burlesque performance pretend to bring a cup of wine to the pretender king. Ironically Jesus truly bears the titles they denied to him. Unwittingly their taunt for Jesus to save himself gets right to the heart of the gospel paradox. For if Jesus does yield to the temptation to save himself by holding on to his life (9:24; see

4:1–13), he will not be able to accomplish God's plan of redeeming those he was sent to save. Though publicly dishonored, humiliated, and abused, Jesus remains faithful to his mission, ever obedient to the will of the Father.

Jesus' fidelity did have a positive effect on one of the criminals. Taking responsibility for his own misdeeds, this repentant sinner proclaimed Jesus' innocence, again sounding one of Luke's central themes. In asking Jesus to remember him in his kingdom, this good thief acknowledged Jesus as the royal Messiah. Jesus offers him immediate salvation, promising him a place in paradise today where he will be with Jesus forever. Originally a name for a delightful garden, in scripture paradise designated the original creation at the Garden of Eden and later became a symbol of the afterlife where the righteous would dwell with God.

Death of Jesus (23:44–56)

[44] It was now about noon and darkness came over the whole land until three in the afternoon [45] because of an eclipse of the sun. Then the veil of the temple was torn down the middle. [46] Jesus cried out in a loud voice, "Father, into your hands I commend my spirit"; and when he had said this he breathed his last. [47] The centurion who witnessed what had happened glorified God and said, "This man was innocent beyond doubt." [48] When all the people who had gathered for this spectacle saw what had happened, they returned home beating their breasts; [49] but all his acquaintances stood at a distance, including the women who had followed him from Galilee and saw these events.

[50] Now there was a virtuous and righteous man named Joseph who, though he was a member of the council, [51] had not consented to their plan of action. He came from the Jewish town of Arimathea and was awaiting the kingdom of God. [52] He went to Pilate and asked for the body of Jesus. [53] After he had taken the body down, he wrapped it in a linen

cloth and laid him in a rock-hewn tomb in which no one had yet been buried. [54] It was the day of preparation, and the sabbath was about to begin. [55] The women who had come from Galilee with him followed behind, and when they had seen the tomb and the way in which his body was laid in it, [56] they returned and prepared spices and perfumed oils. Then they rested on the sabbath according to the commandment.

As sometimes happens at the death of a great person, Jesus' death was marked by two extraordinary signs, one cosmic and the other religious. Both God's creation and the Jewish temple reverberate. Darkness at midday symbolizes the Day of Judgment and the power of evil (Jl 2:1–14; Am 8:9; see 1:79). With his end rapidly approaching, Jesus entrusts himself completely into God's hands invoking the words of Psalm 31:6 (23:46). Having received the Holy Spirit at baptism confirming him as God's son (3:22), Jesus entrusts his own spirit to the Father, saying "Into your hands I commend my spirit." This is surely one of the most meaningful prayers a disciple of Jesus can utter as death draws near.

Jesus' fidelity to God at his death evokes four exemplary responses. The first is from a Gentile, a centurion who had witnessed all that happened. He responds positively to the divine revelation in Jesus by glorifying God (23:47). After Pilate, Herod, and the good thief, he becomes the fourth person who proclaims Jesus' innocence. The second receptive response comes from the people and some of Jesus' acquaintances who behold in a favorable way all these events (23:48–49).

A third positive reaction comes from Joseph of Arimathea, who represents at least one member of the Sanhedrin who had not consented to hand Jesus over to Pilate (23:50–53). Described as a righteous man, he was a devout Jew who awaited the kingdom of God (see 2:25, 36–38). Acting against the common practice of denying a decent burial to an executed criminal, Joseph shows great dignity toward the body of Jesus by wrapping it in linen and placing it in an unused tomb. The fourth positive response comes from the group of Galilean women who had faithfully followed Jesus throughout his journey (23:54–56, see 8:2–3). They observed where Jesus was buried and went to prepare spices and perfumed oils for his body.

The Resurrection of Jesus (23:56b–24:12)

Luke concludes his Gospel with a marvelous series of inter-connected stories that occur on one momentous day, a day centered on the resurrection of Jesus. At the heart of this chapter is the well-acclaimed account of the two travelers on the road to Emmaus. This moving narrative makes up one half of Luke's final chapter, and will be the last story upon which we will reflect.

The five interrelated resurrection events are: 1) the story of the women at the empty tomb, who become the first witnesses to the risen Lord (23:56b–24:12); 2) the appearance of a stranger to two forlorn disciples who recognize him as Jesus at the meal scene in Emmaus (24:13–35); 3) Jesus' appearance to the disciples who are gathered together in Jerusalem (24:36–43); 4) Jesus' final instructions to the disciples who are witnesses to these things (24:44–49); and finally, 5) a brief account of Jesus' ascension into heaven (24:50–53), an event that will be recounted at the beginning of Acts (1:9–10).

All these events take place in and around Jerusalem, in accord with Luke's theological geography. Jerusalem was the destination of the travel narrative and the place where Jesus dies. It is fitting then that Jerusalem be the locale where the resurrected Jesus appears. Jerusalem is the center for the salvation event. It is in that city that the eyewitnesses to the drama of salvation will be transformed through their experience of the living Jesus into a community of ministers of the word (see 1:2). Hence, it is not surprising that Luke begins his second volume with a Jerusalem setting. For it is Luke's vision that the Jesus movement spread through its witnesses, the disciples, from Jerusalem, to

Judea and Samaria, and finally to the ends of the earth (Acts 1:8).

Two other themes run through Luke 24 linking the rich collection of Easter stories. One is the motif of promise and fulfillment. All that Moses, the prophets, and Jesus himself have said comes to pass. It was necessary that the Son of Man, the Messiah, should suffer so as to enter into his glory (24:6–7, 25–27, 44–47). A second theme is that the resurrection events including the appearances of Jesus and the meals with him form a community of believers out of the bewildered followers. Through their experience of the risen Jesus a community of faith is born.

23:56b Then they rested on the sabbath according to the commandment.

24:1 But at daybreak on the first day of the week they took the spices they had prepared and went to the tomb. 2 They found the stone rolled away from the tomb; 3 but when they entered, they did not find the body of the Lord Jesus. 4 While they were puzzling over this, behold, two men in dazzling garments appeared to them. 5 They were terrified and bowed their faces to the ground. They said to them, "Why do you seek the living one among the dead? 6 He is not here, but he has been raised. Remember what he said to you while he was still in Galilee, 7 that the Son of Man must be handed over to sinners and be crucified, and rise on the third day." 8 And they remembered his words. 9 Then they returned from the tomb and announced all these things to the eleven and to all the others. 10 The women were Mary Magdalene, Joanna, and Mary the mother of James; the others who accompanied them also told this to the apostles, 11 but their story seemed like nonsense and they did not believe them. 12 But Peter got up and ran to the tomb, bent down, and saw the burial cloths alone; then he went home amazed at what had happened.

As darkness first gives way to light on the first day of the week, the day after the sabbath rest, a group of women make their way to the tomb. They know where to go for they have witnessed where his body was laid (23:55). We know that these women had come from Galilee although they will not be named until v. 10. Their purpose is simply to anoint the body of Jesus with prepared spices and perfumed oils as was the custom at the time (23:56; 24:1). When they arrived they found that the stone had been rolled back. They enter and observe that the body of Jesus is not there, a fact later verified by Peter (24:12).

Although the women were puzzled by the empty tomb, this itself does not lead to insight or faith in the resurrection. What they observe has to be interpreted. This is done by two men, who though not identified—later they are referred to as angels (24:23)—appear in dazzling garments. The same Greek participle, translated here as "dazzling," is used to describe Jesus' clothes at the transfiguration when he is in his glory (9:29). The mention of two men at the tomb also recalls Moses and Elijah at the transfiguration who are introduced in the same way: "behold, two men" (9:30). At significant revelatory events in Luke two heavenly figures are there to interpret what takes place (see also Acts 1:10).

The question addressed to the women, "Why do you seek the living one among the dead?" comes across as a mild rebuke. Yet, this question, followed by the affirmation that "he has been raised" and the command to recall what Jesus said in Galilee, prompt the women to remember. Hearing this and remembering, they are no longer terrified (24:8). In saying that the women recall "his words," Luke tells us that they came to believe. Remembering is used here in the rich Biblical sense of realizing that Jesus' past words and actions have a significant connection to the present (see 1:54, 72; 23:42; Acts 10:31; 11:16). The women are asked to think back specifically to the saying about the Son of Man, a flashback to the passion predictions (9:22, 44).

Unlike the ending to the resurrection story in Mark's Gospel where the women flee in bewilderment saying nothing to anyone (Mk 16:8), the women in Luke announce to the Eleven and the others what they experienced (24:9). Thus, they become the first to proclaim the resurrection. Their eagerness to share the good news recalls the enthusiastic response of the shepherds in the infancy narrative to what they had seen and heard (2:20). The women in Luke then related their resurrection experience to the apostles (24:10). Giving no credence to these women, the apostles dismissed their story as a tall tale (literally, "nonsense").

Even though these women had faithfully accompanied Jesus from Galilee to Golgotha while the other disciples had fled far from the scene, their witness to the Eleven was rejected. Two obstacles prevent the apostles from hearing the good news. One is that from a cultural perspective women were not viewed as credible witnesses, as reflected by the air of superiority from the male disciples. The second obstacle is that the apostles were still stuck in disbelief. They remained at the same place they were earlier in the narrative, unable to understand (see 9:45; 18:34).

At least one of the apostles, however, was curious enough about the women's message to check out the scene. This was Peter. The last we heard about him was his threefold denial of Jesus after which he wept bitterly (22:62). By running to the tomb, entering and seeing only the burial cloths, Peter takes a positive step though he still does not believe. That will not happen until the Lord appears to him (24:34).

For reflection: The resurrection of Jesus is God's powerful statement that evil and death do not have the last word. God did not abandon Jesus on the cross, just as God does not forget any of the faithful who struggle to follow their Lord. It is easy to become disheartened by looking around at all that is not right with our world, the violence and the hatred, the despair and the evil. Through the resurrection of Jesus, God proclaims that out of darkness comes light, out of despair comes hope, and out of death comes life.

The women do not come to experience the joy of the resurrection without entering the darkness of the tomb. There in the shadows they come to grips with their own doubts and fears. For us to make progress on our spiritual journey it is necessary to embrace our own darkness before we come into the light. And that light has as its source the Risen Christ.

Sometimes that journey from darkness to light is facilitated by an unexpected word or a gesture by a person who cares. Who in your life has been a living witness of Easter joy? Are you sometimes like the apostles who hear words of hope as so much nonsense, or are you open to the unsuspecting, yet marvelous ways that God breaks into life?

Having heard that Jesus was not to be found in the tomb, that he is risen, the women remembered, and came to believe. Acting in faith, they proclaimed "all these things" to the disbelieving disciples. These women were indeed the first apostles of the resurrection. Today as a faith community we are still struggling to understand what this means in regard to women's proper role in the church. To what extent is the faith community able to listen receptively to their experiences of faith? To what extent is their witness regarded as so much nonsense? To live the Easter faith we as believers are challenged not only to be aware of our own experience of the risen Lord but also to be receptive to the faith experience of others in the same risen Lord.

The Emmaus Story (24:13–35)

[13] Now that very day two of them were going to a village seven miles from Jerusalem called Emmaus, [14] and they were conversing about all the things that had occurred. [15] And it happened that while they were conversing and debating, Jesus himself drew near and walked with them, [16] but their eyes were prevented from recognizing him. [17] He asked them, "What are you discussing as you walk along?" They stopped, looking downcast. [18] One of them, named Cleopas, said to him in reply, "Are you the only visitor to Jerusalem who does not know of the things that have taken place there in these days?" [19] And he replied to them, "What sort of things?" They

said to him, "The things that happened to Jesus the Nazarene, who was a prophet mighty in deed and word before God and all the people, [20] how our chief priests and rulers both handed him over to a sentence of death and crucified him. [21] But we were hoping that he would be the one to redeem Israel; and besides all this, it is now the third day since this took place. [22] Some women from our group, however, have astounded us: they were at the tomb early in the morning [23] and did not find his body; they came back and reported that they had indeed seen a vision of angels who announced that he was alive. [24] Then some of those with us went to the tomb and found things just as the women had described, but him they did not see." [25] And he said to them, "Oh, how foolish you are! How slow of heart to believe all that the prophets spoke! [26] Was it not necessary that the Messiah should suffer these things and enter into his glory?" [27] Then beginning with Moses and all the prophets, he interpreted to them what referred to him in all the scriptures. [28] As they approached the village to which they were going, he gave the impression that he was going on farther. [29] But they urged him, "Stay with us, for it is nearly evening and the day is almost over." So he went in to stay with them. [30] And it happened that, while he was with them at table, he took bread, said the blessing, broke it, and gave it to them. [31] With that their eyes were opened and they recognized him, but he vanished from their sight. [32] Then they said to each other, "Were not our hearts burning [within us] while he spoke to us on the way and opened the scriptures to us?" [33] So they set out at once and returned to Jerusalem where they found gathered together the eleven and those with them [34] who were saying, "The Lord has truly been raised and has appeared to Simon!" [35] Then the two recounted what had taken place on the way and how he was made known to them in the breaking of the bread.

The Emmaus story readily inspires, engages, and challenges making it a real literary masterpiece. Striking among the narrative tools Luke employs to create this compelling drama is the double irony of the "informed" disciples telling the "uninformed" stranger, whom they do not recognize as Jesus, about Jesus (24:19–20), and then the "uninformed" stranger enlightening the "informed" disciples (24:25–27).

In this compelling drama Luke paints a colorful canvas with rich "novelistic" touches such as the sadness (24:17), the diminished hope (24:21), the astonishment (24:22), the slowness of heart (24:25), and the burning hearts (24:32) of the disciples. Further, Luke underscores the tension between the companions by his choice of verbs: when Jesus drew near they were "conversing and debating" among themselves (24:15); then Jesus asks them about the words they were "exchanging" (literally, "throwing against") with each other (24:17). This was no ordinary conversation. Luke also has Jesus introduce his teaching with a chiding, emotionally charged epithet, "Oh, how foolish you are!" (24:25). He later reveals Jesus' internal disposition, noting that he acted as if he were going further (24:28).

In their own way the Emmaus travelers have some insight about the true identity of Jesus the Nazarene. They know that he was "a prophet mighty in deed and word before God and all the people" (24:19). They had hoped that he would be the one to redeem Israel—understanding redemption as a political liberation from their oppressors. These companions were all too painfully aware that this would-be Savior had been handed over by some of their own chief priests and rulers, and then put to death. Although the text does not specify, they presumably thought he was put to death by the foreign power that occupied their land, the Romans.

Furthermore, the two disciples had heard the women's report of the empty tomb and their announcement that Jesus was alive. Though astonished by the women's account, they still do not believe. At that moment the stranger begins to explain that the Messiah had to suffer before he could enter into glory. This unrecognized companion also broke open the scriptures for them interpreting the many passages from Moses and the prophets that referred to the Messiah. Later, the two disciples realize that as the scriptures were being explained their hearts were burning within them.

Being invited to join them at their home in Emmaus for an evening meal, the invited stranger becomes the host by taking the bread, blessing it, and sharing it with them. Recalling the Last Supper and especially the multiplication of the loaves, these actions open the eyes of the two travelers to the presence of the risen Lord. But as soon as they recognize him, Jesus vanishes from their sight. The living Jesus is present to them in the breaking of the bread, making this a eucharistic meal.

So now the Emmaus travelers do what the women at the tomb did earlier that Easter day. Returning to Jerusalem they recount to the Eleven all that had happened along their journey and how Jesus was made known to them in the breaking of bread.

For reflection: This meditation, longer than the rest, will focus on seven themes that emerge from this moving story: journey, hospitality, christology, eucharist, evangelization, faith, and story.

Journey: With regard to the journey motif we are invited to identify with the disciples and to reflect on our own life journey. What "strangers" and unexpected experiences have come along our way that have at first seemed to be disconcerting and contrary to expectations? But then, upon later reflection, did we come to see these events with "opened eyes" as manifestations of the Risen One? In following the disciples on the Emmaus journey, we are reminded that it was their mistaken certitude in having a true and complete knowledge of who Jesus is that prevented them from recognizing him. On our own journey let us be open to the unexpected stranger who arrives on the scene as well as to the unanticipated life experiences that unfold. May we ponder these in light of the Christ event.

Hospitality: Even before they recognized the stranger, the disciples were concerned about his welfare, and thus invited him to join them for food and fellowship around the table. It was through their openness to caring for his needs that they were profoundly changed by him. By the offer of hospitality the Emmaus companions transcended their self-concern and sadness, their foolishness and slowness of heart, thus preparing them for the revelatory experience around the table where they were nourished. This passage is a dramatic reminder for us to "not neglect hospitality, for through it some have unknowingly entertained angels" (Heb 13:2). Sometimes the "strangers" to whom hospitality is to be extended may be those who have become estranged for one reason or another from their own community of faith. This story challenges us to find ways to extend hospitality to those who have been excluded from rather than welcomed to the banquet of the Lord.

Christology: This passage provides us with the essential elements for developing a well-grounded understanding of who Christ is. These include: an awareness that Jesus is "a prophet mighty in word and deed" (24:19), that he suffered and died so as to enter into his glory (24:20, 26), that he is not to be found in the tomb for his is "alive" (24:23), that the events about Jesus can only be understood in light of all of scripture (24:27, 32), that his presence is experienced in the breaking of bread (24:30–31, 35), and that he is the heart of the community of believers (24:36–49). United with members of the community, from the day of Emmaus up to the present, we can experience the risen Lord when we gather for "the breaking of bread."

Eucharist: The Emmaus meal clearly recalls the feeding of the five thousand and very probably the Last Supper as well. While at table the traveling disciples come to recognize Jesus in "the breaking of the bread." More than a simple meal of fellowship, this is a sharing of Eucharist. As Acts makes clear, from this moment on the resurrected Jesus, soon to become physically absent after the ascension, will be experienced as present among the community of believers in the breaking of bread. Are we able to recognize the Risen Lord in "the breaking of bread" and in the gathered community of faithful? Do we then go forth and witness to the living Jesus by the way we live?

Evangelizing: Witnessing is made effective by meaningfully connecting these elements: a) knowing and sharing the events about Jesus encompassing his powerful words and deeds, his suffering and death, and the empty tomb and appearances; b) remembering the words of Jesus; and c) explaining the significance of these events and words in light of scripture. This is the model for witnessing that is portrayed in Luke's account of the early church (see e.g., Acts 3:11–26). Any effort that aspires to move immediately from an account of the wondrous deeds of Jesus to redemption for all without considering the necessity of his rejection, suffering and death, falls far short of authentically proclaiming the Risen One. Do we readily embrace the cross while keeping our focus on the living Jesus?

Faith as Sight: A prominent theme in the story is that of faith understood as "sight." At the beginning of his Gospel, Luke has Zechariah, filled with the Holy Spirit, proclaim that "the daybreak from on high will visit us to shine on those who sit in darkness and death's shadow, to guide our feet into the path of peace" (1:78–79), and then Simeon announces that his "eyes have seen your [God's] salvation . . . a light for revelation to the Gentiles" (2:30–32). Although Jesus is physically present to the Emmaus disciples, they are unable to see him for they do not understand the scriptures. Only after they listen to Jesus explain the Torah and are present with him in the breaking of the bread do they come to "see" Jesus. Then, they become aware that their hearts were burning. We move from doubt to faith when we are able to "see" Jesus through the scriptures, in the breaking of the bread, and in the community of faith.

Engaging the Story: As Luke himself does especially well, we are born to tell stories. It is by recounting our experiences to someone willing to listen that meaning emerges, insight is gained, and our lives are changed. In many ways the episode models the qualities of a helpful pastoral conversation. Jesus begins by listening, not by teaching, and thus the Emmaus disciples, confused and searching, entrust him with their story—a story of sadness and grief. By assuming an almost child-like innocence, Jesus asks open-ended questions that invite the two travelers to tell of their dashed hopes and the confusing reports they had heard. Only after Jesus has listened closely to their story, does he respond by interpreting their experiences with reference to the scriptures. In this way Jesus brought about new possibilities for them to reconfigure their lives, thus restoring their lost hope.

With whom do we share our story, our hopes and aspirations, our grief and sadness, our journey of faith? Do we invite others to share their story, offering a caring heart and a non-judgmental presence? Are we able to listen closely to the many, even surprising ways that the risen Lord is present in those around us?

For Further Reading

Craddock, Fred B. *Luke*. Interpretation. Louisville: John Knox, 1990.
Danker, Frederick W. *Jesus and the New Age: A Commentary on St. Luke's Gospel*. Philadelphia: Fortress, rev. ed, 1988.
Fitzmyer, Joseph A. *The Gospel According to Luke*. Anchor Bible. 2 volumes. Garden City, NY: Doubleday, 1981, 1985.
_____. *Luke the Theologian. Aspects of His Teaching*. New York: Paulist Press, 1989.
Gillman, John. *Possessions and the Life of Faith*. Zacchaeus Studies. Collegeville, MN: The Liturgical Press, 1991.
Green, Joel B. *The Gospel of Luke*. The New International Commentary of the New Testament. Grand Rapids, MI: Eerdmans, 1997.
Johnson, Luke Timothy. *The Gospel of Luke*. Sacra Pagina. Collegeville, MN: The Liturgical Press, 1991.
Karris, Robert J. "The Gospel According to Luke." In *The New Jerome Biblical Commentary*, edited by Raymond E. Brown, Joseph A. Fitzmyer, and Roland E. Murphy. Pp. 675–721. Englewood Cliffs, NJ: Prentice Hall, 1990.
_____. *Invitation to Luke*. Garden City, NY: Image Books, 1977.
LaVerdiere, Eugene. *Luke*. New Testament Message. Wilmington, Delaware: Michael Glazier, 1980.
Malina, Bruce J., and Richard L. Rohrbaugh. *Social-Science Commentary on the Synoptic Gospels*. Minneapolis, MN: Fortress, 1992.
Marshall, I. Howard. *The Gospel of Luke: A Commentary on the Greek Text*. New International Greek Testament Commentary. Grand Rapids, MI: Eerdmans, 1978.
Moxnes, H. *The Economy of the Kingdom: Social Conflict and Economic Relations in Luke's Gospel*. Overtures to Biblical Theology. Philadelphia: Fortress, 1988.
Neyrey, Jerome H. (ed.). *The Social World of Luke-Acts. Models for Interpretation*. Peabody, MA: Hendrickson, 1991.
Nolland, John. *Luke*. Word Biblical Commentary. 3 volumes. Dallas, TX: Word, 1989, 1993.
Reid, Barbara. *Choosing the Better Part? Women in the Gospel of Luke*. Collegeville, MN: The Liturgical Press, 1966.

Seim, Turid Karlsen. "The Gospel of Luke." In *Searching the Scriptures. Vol. 2, A Feminist Commentary*, edited by Elisabeth Schüssler Fiorenza, 728–762. New York: Crossroads, 1994.

Tannehill, Robert C. *Luke*. Abingdon New Testament Commentaries. Nashville: Abingdon Press, 1996.

———. *The Narrative Unity of Luke-Acts. A Literary Interpretation. Vol. 1. The Gospel according to Luke*. Philadelphia: Fortress, 1986.

In the Same Series from New City Press

Mark
From Death to Life
Dennis Sweetland
ISBN 1-56548-117-8, paper, 5 3/8 x 8 1/2, 216 pp.

Matthew
God With Us
Ronald D. Witherup
ISBN 1-56548-123-2, paper, 5 3/8 x 8 1/2, 216 pp.

Romans
The Good News According to Paul
Daniel Harrington
ISBN 1-56548-096-1, paper, 5 3/8 x 8 1/2, 152 pp.

First Corinthians
Building Up the Church
Vincent P. Branick
ISBN 1-56548-162-3, paper, 5 3/8 x 8 1/2, 152 pp.

Paul's Prison Letters
On Paul's Letters to Philemon, the Philippians, and the Colossians
Daniel Harrington
ISBN 1-56548-088-0, paper, 5 3/8 x 8 1/2, 136 pp.

Revelation
The Book of the Risen Christ
Daniel Harrington
ISBN 1-56548-121-6, paper, 5 3/8 x 8 1/2, 168 pp.

To Order Phone 1-800-462-5980
www.newcitypress.com

In the Same Series from New City Press

Song of Songs
The Love Poetry of Scripture
Dianne Bergant
ISBN 1-56548-100-3, paper, 5 3/8 x 8 1/2, 168 pp.

Daniel
A Book for Troubling Times
Alexander A. Di Lella
ISBN 1-56548-087-2, paper, 5 3/8 x 8 1/2, 232 pp.

To Order Phone 1-800-462-5980
www.newcitypress.com